# MAKING PLANS

Roger Fullington Series in Architecture

# MAKING PLANS

## HOW TO ENGAGE WITH LANDSCAPE, DESIGN, AND THE URBAN ENVIRONMENT

Frederick R. Steiner

UNIVERSITY OF TEXAS PRESS | AUSTIN

Publication of this book was made possible in part by support from Roger Fullington and
a challenge grant from the National Endowment for the Humanities.

Excerpt from Malcolm X, *By Any Means Necessary: Speeches, Interviews, and a Letter by Malcolm X*
(New York: Pathfinder, 1970); copyright © 1970, 1992 by Betty Shabazz and Pathfinder Press,
reprinted by permission.

Excerpt from Robert Smithson, "A Sedimentation of the Mind: Earth Projects," in *Robert Smithson:
The Collected Writings*, ed. Jack Flam, text copyright © Holt-Smithson Foundation/licensed by
VAGA, New York, NY.

Excerpt from interview on *Qu'est ce que le design* (1972), with Charles Eames, copyright © 2017
Eames Office, LLC (eamesoffice.com).

Excerpt from Louis Kahn, "Order and Form," *Perspecta* 3 (1955): 46–63; courtesy of MIT Press.

Excerpt from Terry Tempest Williams, *Refuge: An Unnatural History of Family and Place*, copyright
© 1991 by Terry Tempest Williams. Used by permission of Pantheon Books, an imprint of the
Knopf Doubleday Publishing Group, a division of Penguin Random House LLC. All rights reserved.

Excerpt from Peter Drucker, *Managing Oneself*; copyright © Drucker 1996 Literary Works Trust,
used by permission.

Requests for permission to reproduce material from this work
should be sent to:
Permissions
University of Texas Press
P.O. BOX 7819
Austin, TX 78713-7819
utpress.utexas.edu/rp-form

Library of Congress Cataloging-in-Publication Data

Names: Steiner, Frederick R., author.

Title: Making plans : how to engage with landscape, design, and the
urban environment / Frederick R. Steiner.

Description: First edition. | Austin : University of Texas Press, 2018. |
Includes bibliographical references and index.

Identifiers: LCCN 2017018217 | ISBN 978-1-4773-1430-2 (cloth : alk. paper) |
ISBN 978-1-4773-1431-9 (pbk : alk. paper) | ISBN 978-1-4773-1432-6 (library e-book) |
ISBN 978-1-4773-1433-3 (nonlibrary e-book)

Subjects: LCSH: City planning. | Regional planning. | Land use—Planning. |
Landscape architecture. | Human ecology.

Classification: LCC HT166 .S684 2018 | DDC 307.1/216—dc23

LC record available at https://lccn.loc.gov/2017018217

doi:10.7560/314302

Dedicated to the memory of

# Kent Butler,

a pioneer in environmental planning

# CONTENTS

# ILLUSTRATIONS AND TABLES

**Figures**

**Tables**

**Boxes**

# MAKING PLANS

# INTRODUCTION

## A PLANNING SPECIES

Our species plans. That's who we humans are: plan makers. We rely on knowledge, experience, instincts, and at times gut reactions to guide our decisions. My ideal kind of plan relies on a careful reading of a place and the situation at hand. Plans require context and vision to provide the connection between what we know and what we want to do. I concur with John Friedmann (1987) that knowledge should lead to action, as well as with Patrick Geddes (1915), who placed diagnosis before treatment. Understanding should precede intervention. Furthermore, I believe plans work best when they are flexible and capable of adjusting to changing circumstances and new information. From nature, we know that it is neither always the strongest of species that survives nor the most intelligent. Rather, it is the species that is most adaptable to change.[1]

Thankfully, we humans are an adaptive species. We can heat our homes in the winter, cool them in the summer, extend light deep into the night, and transmit messages across vast spaces.

Planning is among our most powerful tools for adaptation. Planning is simply thinking ahead. Community and regional planning involves thinking ahead and formally envisioning the future for ourselves and others. These two scales—local and regional—suggest that planners deal with both close-knit groups and larger populations. Environmental and social concerns are equally important at both scales.

I am a planner. With four advanced degrees in planning, I have helped to make many plans since 1970 and have taught planning since 1977. I have worked across the nation, for public agencies and private firms, as well as nonprofits and the federal agencies, including a short stint with the National Park Service. My life began in Ohio, and my plans have taken me to Kentucky, Pennsylvania, the Pacific Northwest, New England, the Front Range, the Southwest, Texas, and back to Pennsylvania. Internationally, my academic pursuits have led me to the Netherlands, Italy, Mexico, Spain, China, Ireland, and Montenegro, among other places. Along the way, I have accumulated lots of ideas about planning.

Ideas put to action generate plans. We want to achieve something and then decide what it will take to get there. In my discipline of community and regional planning, we seek to design the use of land and create better places for people to live. Increasingly, we incorporate the quality of other species' habitat as well. For instance, Marcus Owens and Jennifer Wolch (2015) have urged us to theorize about a "more-than-human city." Similarly, Timothy Beatley (2010, 2016) and others have advocated "biophilic cities." The welfare of other species, and nature generally, are regarded as essential for happy, healthy, and meaningful human lives in such cities.

A genesis decision point occurs between the idea of planning a place and setting goals. This pivot point marks a transition from an individual idea to a commitment to community ideas. Once that decision is made, we begin planning by setting goals, that is, stating where we want to go as a community. With a land-use plan, for example, our goal might be to develop certain areas of a city or a county for affordable housing, while preserving other places for wildlife habitat. Goals are often linked with objectives, or the steps necessary to take us where we want to go. With my kind of plan, setting objectives comes later in the process, when we select a course of action.

After we establish goals, we need to take stock of what we have. A landscape is the synthesis of the natural and social phenomena that compose a place. We can understand our communities and regions by learning to read landscapes. Ecology is the science that can advance such literacy because it involves understanding the relationships of all organisms, including us humans, to each other and our environments. By extension, our human ecology has far-reaching consequences. As Pope Francis has observed, "Human ecology is inseparable from the notion of common good, a central and underlying principle of social ethics" (2015, 156).

Through reading landscapes ecologically, we can discover that some places are better suited for specific uses than others, often economically and socially as well as environmentally. Certain uses may seem to belong to a location naturally or be essential to a place. Such uses are intrinsic.

In contrast, some places are downright dangerous for certain human uses. For instance, we know that floodplains sometimes fill up with water, at times quite rapidly. If we allow houses, town centers, or schools to locate (and to relocate) in flood-prone places, people are put in harm's way. Likewise, we know that earthquakes can injure and kill people and result in property damage. Common sense suggests that a known and active fault zone is an unwise location for a nuclear power plant. We have the knowledge to minimize harm by locating some development away from floodplains and fault zones and storm-surge areas and places susceptible to wildfire. We can also design buildings and landscapes that limit structural damage and minimize risk to people and other life-forms. When homes and neighborhoods are submerged by floodwaters or torn apart by an earthquake, our hearts go out to the victims. We should display similar compassion and prevent people from locating settlements in dangerous places. Furthermore, the costs of not assessing the suitability or the fitness of a parcel of land for possible uses can result in sprawling and ineffective infrastructure. Associated maintenance costs over time can far exceed expectations. Often, unsuitable land uses are just plain inefficient and/or inconvenient.

Many areas are suitable for several uses. Flat land is often good for farming and urban development. This book provides examples of how various options for uses can be explored and how land-use policy conflicts can be resolved (or at least acknowledged). Such investigation involves weighing the costs and the benefits for each option as well as identifying who are the potential winners and losers from various paths of action. The idea is to maximize the benefits for the public good while limiting negative impacts. We make decisions based on analyzing the various options that lie ahead. A trend is a consequence not of destiny but of the choices we make through planning.

Planning options can be informed through design experiments that explore the spatial consequences of actions; by analysis, such as the reading of the landscape through an ecological lens; and from projections of population, transportation demand, and the economy. While analysis is most helpful, it is not by itself planning.

Design gives form to planning ideas. Design can help those who are impacted by various planning possibilities to visualize and understand environment, development, population growth or decline, and transportation impacts and possibilities. This and the remaining steps in the planning process are often more an art than a science. While creativity is an asset, these steps should also be undertaken with the knowledge of law, precedent, design, finance, and urban history. For the remaining steps, effective planners function more like designers—landscape architects and architects—than applied social scientists.

After preferred options are determined, including the possibility of inaction, planners establish objectives that outline the specific measures necessary to accomplish the goals for the plan. This step might involve revising or even resetting goals. With goals and objectives in place, a specific course of action can be determined and then pursued. This might involve enacting a regulation (for instance, no houses in the floodplain) or designing a new park (for instance, put the park in the floodplain). The actions may be bold or modest.

As we take actions to achieve our goals and objectives, we need to remain flexible and be capable of adjusting to change. For example, a dam or a diversion tunnel might alter the floodplain for a river or stream. As a result, we may rethink where the best spots for houses and for parks are located. Global climate change is also affecting landscapes as biomes migrate toward the poles, the ranges of the bumblebee shrink, and fruit trees flower unseasonably earlier. Through planning, we can better adapt to change. Plans need to be adjustable to changing conditions. This requires that planning and plans be time-sensitive, dynamic, and adaptable by design.

I believe in democracy. As a consequence, I think it is essential for citizens to participate in making plans. The public should help set goals and objectives, read landscapes, determine best uses, design options, select courses for moving forward, take actions, and adjust to changes. Planning is a political act and as such requires the intelligence and ownership of impacted communities. Citizens cannot do it all; that is why communities retain planners. We are expected to bring expertise to the process. This requires more than attending meetings and recording citizen preferences (though this can be of help). We are expected to bring knowledge and imagination to the plan-making process.

We need to produce better plans for our communities, cities and towns, and regions. Improved plans can lead to healthier, safer, and more beautiful places for us and other species to live. We can also plan for places that are both more just and more profitable. Plans can help us not only to sustain what we value but also to transcend sustainability by creating truly regenerative communities, that is, places with the capacity to restore, renew, and revitalize their own sources of energy and materials.

However, in reality, nothing ever goes exactly as planned. Plan making is a human endeavor, and human nature is a tangled, wonderful mess. I began writing this book while engaged in two plans in Austin. My activity in both started in 2009 and continued into 2016. One was the city's first comprehensive plan since 1979, and the other was a new campus master plan for the University of Texas at Austin. I was deeply involved in both planning processes. The city council appointed me to serve on the comprehensive plan citizens' advisory task force. At the university, I helped write the proposal that led to the plan and cochaired the campus plan advisory committee. In both cases, I remained involved throughout the process. As the chair of the campus planning committee, I stayed directly engaged in the campus plan and its implementation until I moved to Philadelphia in the summer of 2016. My ongoing involvement with the city was more sporadic, but focused, such as being a member of the Waller Creek Local Government Corporation. The city and campus plans, with others, will be used as reflective examples as we move through the planning process in this book.

This is my kind of plan: a framework that adjusts to what goes awry, but helps move us forward to a better future.

# 1 — SETTING GOALS

## A DECLARATION OF ASPIRATION

The future belongs to those who prepare for it today.
— Malcolm X

We begin with an idea about the future. This might be prompted by some opportunity or some challenge we face. We may be motivated by a vision. Martin Luther King declared, "I have a dream." He then described his goal to achieve that vision. Specifically, "I have a dream that my four little children will one day live in a nation where they will not be judged by the color of their skin but by the content of their character."

John F. Kennedy stated in 1961 that "we choose to go to the moon," adding that the United States would accomplish this by the end of the decade. In response, NASA put in place the goal to achieve a moon landing before 1970. The goal was accomplished when the *Eagle* of the Apollo 11 mission landed on the moon on July 20, 1969, and Neil Armstrong and Buzz Aldrin took their walks on its surface the next day.

Apple cofounder Steve Jobs was direct about the aspiration of his typical employee: "We attract a different type of person—a person who doesn't want to wait five or ten years to have someone take a giant risk on him or her. Someone who really wants to get in a little over his head and make a little dent in the universe."[1] Jobs's goal, like that of his employees, was to change how we communicate.

What if we aren't going to the moon or trying to change the race relationships of a nation or revolutionizing communications? What if we merely seek to better our community? We should still aim high. We should still begin with a compelling vision, something to inspire us. We might begin by seeking to make our community the best possible.

Okay then, what is our community? What is the best?

Umpteen social scientists have defined "community." Basically, it comes down to the people we associate with: the folks who live around us, our coworkers, those who share our beliefs.

"Best" is a bit more slippery.

At the University of Texas, the football team is clear about how to be best: it must be ranked number one at the end of the season. As a result, losing to Notre Dame to start the season is not an auspicious beginning. Moving away from sports across the campus, academic programs would like to be regarded as best, too. However, the ranking of academic programs often seems even more arbitrary[2] than in football, where the highly ranked teams play each other in bowl games (and even then, controversy frequently ensues about the team that emerges on top).

Cities are ranked, too. We rate many aspects of cities: quality of life, infrastructure, foreclosures, safety (and crime), greenness, jobs, affordability, tech savviness, volunteerism, walkability, and so on. Such aspects might find their way into community goals as we strive to improve our quality of life, our infrastructure, our walkability, and so on.

My former home—Austin, Texas—frequently scores high in various city rankings. City leaders often cite these rankings as evidence of success. Are they conscious goals pursued by the city's leaders? Or are they the happy consequence of being home to the state capital and a major university?

What roles do live music, rolling tree-covered hills, and a dammed-up river in the middle of the city play?

Goals can address both the needs and the wants of a city, a community, or a campus. On the one hand, affordable housing may be needed to provide shelter for everyone in a community. On the other hand, citizens may want a new football stadium for their city for a variety of reasons such as civic pride and economic development. Likewise, a university may need more student housing and also want a new sports arena.

## Planning a "Terminally Democratic" but Historically Segregated City (Austin)

Wallace Roberts & Todd (WRT), an urban planning and design firm based in Philadelphia, cooperated with a team of city staff, citizens, and other consultants to produce a new Austin comprehensive plan. The previous comprehensive plan had resulted from the Austin Tomorrow planning process undertaken during the late 1970s. The plan was adopted in 1979 and published in book form in 1980 (City of Austin 1980). WRT, then Wallace, McHarg, Roberts, and Todd (WMRT), had influenced the visionary Austin Tomorrow plan through its 1976 *Lake Austin Growth Management Plan*. But planning has had a long history, some of it especially hideous, in Austin.

In 1839, Judge Edwin Waller created the first plan for the city along the northern banks of the Colorado River. He used the ridge line between Shoal Creek to the west and what would be named Waller Creek in his honor to the east to lay out a square-mile (1.6-kilometer) grid of fourteen blocks bisected by a central north-south[3] street named Congress Avenue. The north-south streets parallel to Congress were named for Texas rivers. The east-west streets were originally named for native trees of the region.

Of its several plans, the city's 1928 plan is its most notorious. Completed by the engineers Koch & Fowler, the plan reinforced the segregation of the city. Its authors wrote:

In our studies in Austin we have found that the negroes are present in small numbers, in practically all sections of the city, excepting the area just east of East Avenue and south of the City Cemetery. This area seems to be all negro population. It is our recommendation that the nearest approach to the solution of the race segregation problem will be the recommendation of this district as a negro district; and that all the facilities and conveniences be provided the negroes in this district, as an incentive to draw the negro population to this area. (Koch & Fowler 1928, 57)

Whereas African Americans had been "present in small numbers" throughout the city, the plan included a consensus goal to create a "Negro District" on the east side, which "institutionalized racial segregation by delivering services to minorities in only one section of the city" (Busch 2016, 88). The result was that the city was divided, east and west, black and white, with an additional district for "Mexicans."[4] Separate institutions were created as well, such as the branch library known as the "Colored Branch" until it was renamed the George Washington Carver Branch Library in 1947 and subsequently evolved into an important community museum and cultural center.

Austin's 1928 plan was written in reaction to a 1917 Supreme Court decision (*Buchanan v. Warley*) which held that a Louisville, Kentucky, ordinance prohibiting "Negroes" from living in predominantly "white" areas was unconstitutional. Since black residents could not be prohibited from owning property and living in white areas, the 1928 Austin plan sought to accomplish its goal of segregation through the denial of services. The 1928 plan is widely cited for blatant racism and richly deserves all the scorn it has received, because it helped institutionalize racial segregation in the city, but beyond that it is also a fine example of early twentieth-century plans that primarily focused on the orderly expansion of public infrastructure such as parks and boulevards.

The division fostered by the 1928 plan was reinforced by the construction of Interstate 35 over East Avenue during the 1950s, with the downtown section dedicated in May 1962. Furthermore, Austin's 1961 plan recommended that much of the east side of the city "be destroyed to make room for a large industrial park that would attract business to Austin while displacing thousands of minority residents" (Busch 2016, 90). The racial division finally began to lessen in the 1960s and 1970s, but it still persists to the present.

While the 1979 Austin Tomorrow plan had been effective, it was amended numerous times over the next three decades and clearly needed to be updated to address more current challenges and opportunities. Through the spring and summer of 2009, Austin city planners reached out to the university to engage faculty and students early in the process, beginning in the design phase, or, as they say in Texas, when "we were fixin' to plan." The city had various expectations for the new plan. From the city manager's perspective, the updated plan would be helpful in capital improvement programming and future bond elections. The city planners saw it as an opportunity to produce a "landmark plan" that would address public engagement, sustainability, and implementation. Informed citizens viewed it as an opportunity to address traffic congestion, create more affordable housing, expand parklands, and constrain suburban sprawl.

As with other states, Texas enables municipalities to use their police powers to adopt plans and zoning ordinances to promote public health, safety, morals, and general welfare. Constitutional law in the United States enables states to use such authority to regulate behavior and to enforce order. The Austin city charter requires that the council adopt a plan by ordinance and specifies that it include ten elements to achieve long-range development goals:

1. future land use;
2. traffic circulation and mass transit;
3. wastewater, solid waste, drainage, and potable water;
4. conservation and environmental resources;
5. recreation and open space;
6. housing;
7. public services and facilities, which shall include but not be limited to a capital improvement program;
8. public buildings and related facilities;
9. commercial and industrial development and redevelopment; and
10. health and human services (adapted from City of Austin 2009b, 5).

The definition of these elements in Austin's charter is important. Unlike in other states, Texas planning statutes do not define minimum content for comprehensive plans. This has even resulted in court findings validating citywide zoning maps as comprehensive plans.

The Austin charter's rather generic elements are similar to require-ments for comprehensive and general plans in other jurisdictions across the United States and beyond. In the United States the framework for planning was established in 1928 through the publication of *A Standard City Planning Enabling Act* by Secretary Herbert Hoover's Department of Commerce. According to the enabling act, the plan should include

> careful and comprehensive surveys and studies of present conditions and future growth of the municipality and with due regard to its relation to neighboring territory. The plan shall be made with the general purpose of guiding and accomplishing a coordinated, adjusted, and harmonious development of the municipality and its environs which will, in accor-dance with present and future needs, best promote health, safety, morals, order, convenience, prosperity, and general welfare, as well as efficiency and economy in the process of development; including, among other things, adequate provision for traffic, the promotion of safety from fire and other dangers, adequate provision for light and air, the promotion of the healthful and convenient distribution of population, the promotion of good civic design and arrangement, wise and efficient expenditure of pub-lic funds, and the adequate provision of public utilities and other public requirements. (US Department of Commerce 1928, 16–17)

Note that the authors of the enabling act emphasize that the plan must "promote health, safety, morals, order, convenience, prosperity, and gen-eral welfare." Later in the document, the scope of regional plans was ex-plained to include

> recommendations for the physical development of the region and may include among other things the general location, extent and character of streets, parks and other public ways, grounds and open spaces, pub-lic buildings, and properties and public utilities (whether publicly or privately owned or operated) which affect the development of the region

as a whole or which affect more than one political subdivision of the State within the region; also, the general location of forests, agricultural and open development areas for purposes of conservation, food and water supply, sanitary and drainage facilities, or the protection of future urban development. (US Department of Commerce 1928, 50)

The authors continued by again emphasizing the value of planning for "health, safety, morals, order, convenience, prosperity, and general welfare." The enabling act helped establish the basic foundation for planning elements throughout the United States. In comprehensive or general plans, goals are set for each element.

However, before setting goals for each element, the city council in Austin established three "overarching goals" that would help integrate the elements and distinguish the process: community engagement, sustainability, and implementation. These encompassing goals reflected the planning staff's vision for a landmark plan, one that would be as influential and consequential as Austin Tomorrow. The council explained the process goals as follows:

1. Community Engagement: The planning process will include multiple ways of engaging the public, with the overall goal of developing a plan that reflects the values and aspirations of the entire Austin community.
2. Sustainability: The planning process will define what sustainability means specifically for Austin and the aspirations of Austinites for a sustainable future environment, economy, and community.
3. Implementation: The planning process will incorporate a strategic focus on implementation, culminating in formulation of a realistic action agenda and benchmarks to measure progress in achieving the vision. (City of Austin 2009b, 6)

Two of these overarching goals matched up well with the values of Austin citizens. On the one hand, they do engage in civic activities. While designing the City Hall between 1999 and 2004, the architect Antoine Predock observed that Austinites are "terminally democratic." Many academics, musicians, and politicians call Austin home, and all three groups enjoy performing. Environmentalists wield considerable influence in the city, and environmental quality provides a central tenet of sustainability.

On the other hand, the city does not always follow through in a timely fashion, or at all in some cases. Implementation frequently challenges Austinites. For example, an innovative Great Streets Plan had been prepared for downtown by my colleague Sinclair Black in 2001, but by the time the city council wrote its three overarching process goals in 2009, only one block had been realized. Meanwhile, a commuter rail line remained unopened months after the original date set for its opening.[5] As a result, the establishment of implementation as a priority from the get-go was wise.

In April 2009 the city council selected the WRT team of consultants to assist with the plan. To help WRT and the city's staff to "articulate the common values that will guide Austin into the future," the citizens' advisory committee was organized. WRT suggested an ideal size of twenty to twenty-five members. However, true to its terminally democratic nature, the city council expanded the committee to twenty-nine members, representing university, high school, county, business, open space, bicycle, affordable housing, and other interests. When the city council approved the members on September 24, 2009, it reserved four additional places for county representatives and retained the option of adding more members.

The WRT team (led by David Rouse and John Fernsler, who both resemble slightly disheveled college professors) and the city's staff (led with diligent earnestness by Garner Stoll, Matt Dugan, and Greg Claxton)[6] held numerous events to solicit ideas for the process, which was dubbed "Imagine Austin." The naming of Imagine Austin was itself an exercise in "terminal democracy." The city planning staff developed an interest list of more than two thousand citizens, asked them to suggest names, and held an online election. The winner by a wide margin, selected from the top five names suggested, was "Imagine Austin."

At the first comprehensive plan's kick-off open house on Monday, October 12, 2009, at the Austin Convention Center, 230 citizens viewed demographic and environmental information about the city. They were invited to identify issues that the comprehensive plan should address as well as to express their hopes for its outcome. Forty children engaged in a "kid's plan" and, this being Austin, a series of musicians provided a live soundtrack for the gathering. Six November community forum meetings followed the open house in high schools around the city to discuss "issues and aspirations."

Following the kick-off open house and the first round of community forums, many more meetings and considerable participation ensued: two more community forum series (involving four and nine public meetings), two rounds of citizen surveys, numerous "meetings-in-a-box" (that is, small, self-directed group meetings hosted by individuals, organizations, groups, or businesses with elected officials, staff, or facilitators present), an online survey, and at least once-a-month citizens' task force meetings. The jargony "meetings-in-a-box" small gatherings were renamed "community conversations," for which the city provided invitations, scripts, questions, and directions for returning the results. Meanwhile, the comprehensive plan process appeared frequently on the agendas of the city planning commission and the city council and garnered considerable attention in the local press.

Early in these discussions, the city planners asked the public about Austin's strengths and weaknesses and what the city should be like on its two-hundredth anniversary in 2039. A vision emerged. The city council endorsed the Imagine Austin vision on August 26, 2010, which read, in part,

> As it approaches its 200th anniversary, Austin is a beacon of sustainability, social equity and economic opportunity; where diversity and creativity are celebrated; where community needs and values are recognized; where leadership comes from its citizens and where the necessities of life are affordable and accessible to all. Austin's greatest asset is its people: passionate about our city, committed to its improvement, and determined to see this vision become a reality.

The vision continued with elaborations of seven key principles:

Austin is livable
Austin is natural and sustainable
Austin is mobile and interconnected
Austin is prosperous
Austin values and respects its people
Austin is creative
Austin is educated

Through the process, key "objectives" were attached to each of these principles, as illustrated in box 1, such as that to be livable, Austin must promote healthy and safe communities, and to be prosperous, there must be diverse business opportunities. These are objectives by definition, that is, the targets of actions. In planning, objectives are more specific results that are to be achieved within a specified timeframe with available resources. I would identify the objectives in box 1 as goals.

The new plan was timely because the challenge was clear: the city and the metropolitan region were growing rapidly. In 1990, Austin had 465,622 residents; in 2000, 656,562; and in 2010, 790,390.[7] The city was expected to add between 700,000 and 750,000 more people by 2039. Meanwhile, the metropolitan region now is home to over two million people and is expected to rise to almost four million by 2040.

---

BOX 1. IMAGINE AUSTIN PRINCIPLES AND OBJECTIVES

**Desired characteristics of Austin**

**Livable**
- Healthy and safe communities
- Housing diversity and affordability
- Access to community amenities
- Quality design/distinctive character
- Preservation of crucial resources

**Natural and sustainable**
- Sustainable, compact, and walkable development
- Resource conservation/efficiency
- Extensive green infrastructure

**Creative**
- Vibrant cultural events/programs
- Support for arts/cultural activities

**Educated**
- Learning opportunities for all ages
- Community partnerships with schools
- Relationships with higher learning

**Prosperous**
- Diverse business opportunities
- Technological innovation
- Education/skills development

**Mobile and interconnected**
- Range of transportation options
- Multimodal connectivity
- Accessible community centers

**Values and respects people**
- Access to community services
- Employment and housing options
- Community/civic engagement
- Responsive/accountable government

---

Through the subsequent two and a half years, the citizens' advisory task force would continue to spearhead the community engagement efforts. (For a frank discussion about the benefits and pitfalls of public participation, see Faga 2006). The task force itself would have thirty-one regular meetings, eight special meetings, and sixty-eight committee meetings (table 1). A variety of activities, events, emails, and online polling resulted in more than eighteen thousand comments, believed to have come from several thousand individuals (tables 2 and 3).

TABLE 1. TASK FORCE MEETINGS

| Task force meeting | Number |
|---|---|
| Regular | 31 |
| Special | 8 |
| Steering Committee | 14 |
| Analysis Committee | 10 |
| Communications Committee | 3 |
| Engagement Committee | 10 |
| Joint Committee meetings | |
| Analysis and Communications | 9 |
| Analysis and Engagement | 2 |
| Engagement and Communications | 1 |
| Analysis and PC Comp Plan Committee | 5 |
| Working group cochairs work session | 7 |

TABLE 2. INDIVIDUAL CITIZEN INVOLVEMENT

| Event | Number of participants |
|---|---|
| Participation Plan | 70 |
| Community Forum Series 1 | 5,892 |
| Community Forum Series 2 | 4,211 |
| Community Forum Series 3 | 4,761 |
| Neighborhood Plan meetings | 246 |
| Working groups | 373 |
| Community Forum Series | 2,979 |
| Total participants | 18,532 |

TABLE 3. COMMUNITY ENGAGEMENT ACTIVITIES

| Meeting type | Number of meetings/date (if only one) |
| --- | --- |
| Public Participation Workshop | August 2009 |
| Kick-off open house | October 2009 |
| Community Forum Series 1 | 6 public meetings |
| Community Forum Series 2 | 4 public meetings, 8 follow-on meetings |
| Speak Week | 42 events |
| Community Forum Series 3 | 9 public meetings |
| Taking It to the Streets | 15 events |
| Community meeting on neighborhood plans and comprehensive plan | September 2010 |
| Community meeting on neighborhood plans and comprehensive plan | October 2010 |
| Community meeting with neighborhood plan contact teams | January 2011 |
| Study session on plan framework and preferred growth scenario | February 2011 |
| Working groups | |
|   Orientation | 2 in February/March 2011 |
|   Brainstorming | 7 |
|   Map meetings | 2 |
|   Assessing | 7 |
|   Ranking | 7 |
| Expert panel discussions | |
|   Open Space and Green Infrastructure | |
|   Redevelopment over the Edwards Aquifer | |
|   Connecting State Highway 45 Southwest | |
|   Development in the ETJ, especially along State Highway 130 | |
|   Complete Communities | |
| Transitions/Compatibility | 6 in July/August 2011 |
| Closeout | 1 |
| Community meeting with neighborhood plan contact teams | August 2011 |
| Community Forum Series #4 | 2 public meetings |

These meetings were generally tedious affairs that ground on beyond their scheduled time with sparks of controversy, disagreement, and humor. The task force received time-limited (three minutes) comments from the public, which were frequently incoherent and ill-informed, but occasionally thoughtful and well-prepared. The task force members bickered among ourselves about all types of issues (and nonissues): maps, equity, the wording of all the various materials that we reviewed, the role of consultants, the organization of meetings, our role, past injustices, density, neighborhood plans, traffic, the creative class, skateboarders, light rail, McMansions, music, NIMBYs, water, heat, food trucks, the food available at the meeting, accessory uses, and so on. Our chair, the retired state district judge Margaret Cooper, was skilled at running a courtroom and knowledgeable about Robert's Rules of Order, which had little effectiveness with a group full of rebellious activists. Some task force members listened, but most talked (a lot). Staff members and the consultants attempted to steer the meetings, with more success in the public gatherings than with the task force. After a while, the WRT team stopped flying in from Philadelphia. Their firsthand influence on the task force waned. The consultants continued to work directly with city staff members instead (which, no doubt, had budgetary efficiencies too).

Throughout the extensive public engagement efforts, considerable efforts were employed to involve diverse communities. Overall, the African American and Asian American representation was pretty good; the involvement of Latinos, less so. Still, some small successes occurred. At a workshop early in the process in the Travis High School gymnasium, a group of twelve Hispanic citizens, with limited English abilities, attended. They appeared to be a family with three generations represented. The city staff had not retained translators for this event. My UT planning colleague Patricia Wilson intervened. Fluent in Spanish, Dr. Wilson worked with the group through the evening, and they departed for home quite satisfied. The city did provide written materials in Spanish, had translators at larger events, and targeted Hispanic neighborhoods for involvement activities. Hispanic leaders were also active with the citizens' advisory task force. Still, their involvement did not equal their numbers in the city. In contrast, African Americans and Asian Americans were more engaged and more influential throughout the process. The city hired an African American public participation consultant and the Asian Chamber of Commerce distributed Imagine Austin surveys throughout the process. The Asian Chamber was committed to ensuring there was solid representation from its community. The city spent more resources to boost Hispanic participation, including consultants and translation services, than on any other outreach efforts but still fell short of its goals.

Goals express community aspirations. For Austin, the city council established encompassing process goals. City planners engaged citizens to develop a vision, principles, and objectives. What the Austin city planners called "objectives" formed the principal goals for the comprehensive plan.

## Campus Planning as a Return on Investment (UT Austin)

Soon after the city launched its comprehensive planning process in the summer of 2009, several UT Austin administrators began discussion about a new campus plan. The previous plan had been prepared in 1999 by a team led by Cesar Pelli & Associates (now Pelli Clarke Pelli Architects). The Pelli plan built on a campus planning tradition that had included the important early twentieth-century architects Cass Gilbert and Paul Cret (Cesar Pelli & Associates and Balmori Associates 1999; Speck and Cleary 2011). However, several changes to the campus and emergent issues generated the need for an updated plan. Sustainability and concern about energy conservation had emerged since the Pelli plan. In addition, a Getty Foundation-funded preservation study for the core of the campus and a new landscape plan for the major north-south corridor through the campus (Speedway Mall) illustrated the need for greater attention to conservation and open space concerns. Incremental decisions about new buildings resulted in larger footprints and a steady erosion of the campus landscape, with overall cumulative negative consequences.

In addition, the Commission of 125 had recommended a new campus master plan. The commission had been convened in 2002 by President Larry Faulkner to express a vision of how UT Austin could best serve the state and society during the next twenty-five years. The group included 218 members chosen for occupational, ethnic, and geographic diversity.

Ninety were honorary members who had served as members of the UT System Board of Regents or on one of two previous visioning efforts—the Committee of 75 (which concluded its work in 1958) and the Centennial Commission (1983). Members represented twenty-two states and two foreign countries. The Commission of 125 was chaired by Kenneth M. Jastrow II, chairman and chief executive officer of Temple-Inland.

After nearly two years of deliberations, the commission delivered its report to Faulkner on September 30, 2004. The commission recommended one imperative: "The University of Texas must create a disciplined culture of excellence that will enable it to realize its constitutional mandate." The imperative alludes to the Constitution of the State of Texas, which states, "The Legislature shall . . . establish, organize, and provide for the maintenance, support, and direction of a University of the first class." To that end, the commission made sixteen operational recommendations, of which recommendations five through seven addressed producing a new comprehensive campus master plan. I helped write these recommendations in 2004:

### Recommendation Five

Develop a University Master Plan to integrate academic planning and strategic goals with our facilities, infrastructure, and financial resources. . . .

   The University Master Plan for facilities, infrastructure, and financial resources must serve academic initiatives and aspirations, thereby providing a road map to support a disciplined culture of excellence. . . .

### Recommendation Six

The University must consistently make the best use of its facilities, especially its classroom and laboratory space and off-campus properties, while maintaining a superior campus environment. New facilities should be designed and built more efficiently, with better coordination among academic, facilities planning, operations, and fundraising divisions.

   The University has a backlog of critical maintenance and renovation projects, largely the result of the aging of the campus and inadequate resources. It has neglected open spaces that are vital campus assets. . . .

**Recommendation Seven**

Build financial strength and develop new public and private resources to support academic excellence. . . .

Non-traditional financing can produce benefits and reduce costs in building construction, joint ventures, and auxiliary services. (Commission of 125 2004, 24–26)

For a new plan, Professor Larry Speck and I proposed a novel approach. To prepare the campus plan, we recommended that UT Austin retain a team of School of Architecture faculty members managed by a professional firm rather than hiring an outside consultant. We believed that most of the talent needed for the plan existed within our school and could be augmented with engineering faculty in a few key areas.

Professor Speck and I defined ten task areas—overall goals—for the plan, summarized as follows:

1. Create a complete campus transportation plan that would integrate pedestrian, bicycle, automobile, mass transit, and service vehicle circulation both to and from the campus and within the campus.
2. Create a complete engineering infrastructure plan that would provide projections regarding servicing and utilities requirements for the campus for the foreseeable future.
3. Create a campus hydrology plan along with a specific scheme for enhancement of Waller Creek.[8]
4. Create a sustainability plan for the physical environment of the campus.
5. Create a general landscape plan for the campus. This would not produce detailed landscape design of the sort that landscape architect Peter Walker had done for Speedway Mall and the East Mall; rather, it would create more general policies for campus landscape focused on minimizing water usage and maximizing economy, durability, ease of maintenance, and sustainability, as well as the beauty of campus landscape.[9]
6. Create a historical inventory plan and a preservation/adaptive reuse plan for the campus.[10]

7. Create a unification plan for the campus that would knit back together the portion of the campus to the east of San Jacinto Boulevard/Waller Creek and the portion of the campus to the west of that divide.
8. Create a plan for campus infill and building replacement.
9. Create a plan for housing on campus.
10. Create new design guidelines for building on the campus.

These tasks embed clear goals for the campus plan, that is, they "Create a complete campus transportation plan," "Create a complete engineering infrastructure plan," and so on. In November 2009 we presented these goals to the university's top leaders and posed two basic questions: "How are we using space on campus?" and "How are we spending funds for building projects?"

Larry Speck and I established these ten tasks as goals for the master plan through discussions with relatively few people. We derived the tasks from our own ideas as well as from those of the faculty building advisory committee and responsible university administrators, with suggestions from a few colleagues with specific expertise in historic preservation, transportation, sustainability, and campus planning. By contrast, the Austin plan involved thousands of citizens with scores of opinions and options.

The ten tasks and the approach of employing School of Architecture faculty as campus planners were well received within the university, especially by its president, Bill Powers, and its vice president, Dr. Patricia Clubb. Prior to becoming university president, the Berkeley- and Harvard-educated Powers had been dean of the School of Law and was the author of "The Powers Report," which essentially brought on the final demise of Enron. With a PhD in political science from UT Austin, Clubb was the highly effective maven of the campus's physical infrastructure, from the power plant and parking lots to the buildings and grounds. However, approval by the University of Texas System was necessary. The system had begun to advocate new plans for all its campuses. While the tasks were well received by the system, the approach of an architecture faculty–led plan was not. Pat Clubb devised a compromise that would give more responsibility to an outside coordinating consultant but would still involve university faculty.

We began to prepare a request for qualifications (RFQ) in late spring 2010. How to include or not to include the faculty participants in the RFQ became a sticky issue. In the end, a requirement for faculty participation was not explicitly included, but the consultant was given the role of focusing on the coordination of expertise to undertake the ten tasks and an additional task that indicated how the plan would generate a return on investment (ROI) to the university. The RFQ was issued in July 2010.

Of the firms that responded, we interviewed two finalist teams in September 2010. Both groups were clearly well qualified and experienced. One team took a more traditional campus planning approach, deeply rooted in design; the other offered innovation, with a strong orientation toward metrics. The university selected Sasaki Associates, the innovator, a firm established by the landscape architect and Harvard professor Hideo Sasaki in 1953. Sasaki Associates had developed a space management tool for Ohio State University. This computer-based technique helped Ohio State administrators connect their teaching and research space allocation decisions with its fiscal and facilities planning. Sasaki found that Ohio State's leaders really did not know all the specific uses of their space and whether those uses were efficient. Dr. Clubb observed that we faced a similar situation. She and I worked to convince our leaders about the value of the tool. Our lobbying included a video conference between our leaders and Ohio State's (who all dressed in scarlet and gray; in contrast, we did not don burnt orange for the meeting), as well as a conversation between President Powers and the Buckeye president, Gordon Gee.

While our advocacy helped advance Sasaki's case, their price tag (around $3.5 million) coupled with the slumping economy resulted in caution. Dr. Clubb and I argued that the costs for not planning were even higher and that the ROI of a new campus plan would be high. With Sasaki, we provided examples. Furthermore, the wealthier schools at UT Austin (engineering and business) had undertaken their own plans. If this trend were to continue, the campus could become more balkanized. One of UT Austin's great strengths has been the high level of collegiality and cooperation across the disciplines.

President Powers supported the concept of the plan but asked us to convince him what the ROI would be. The university had dwindling financial support from the state: less than 13 percent of our budget and dropping. As a result, Powers expected an ROI on every activity. He urged the senior staff to read Michael Lewis's *Moneyball* (2003) and act accordingly.

We asked Sasaki if they could reduce the scope and the fees and focus on the ROI. They responded with a list of six tasks and a fee of $1.7 million in March 2011. These six tasks would become what we hoped would constitute the first phase of the plan. Pat Clubb and I anticipated that the results would be so compelling as to prompt a second phase. In addition to reducing the number of tasks, the scope was also narrowed to focus on the campus west of I-35. Relationships between the university and neighborhoods to the east had been strained in the past. Proper planning would require additional funds and time to ensure proper engagement with those communities. The narrower focus included the following six tasks (whittled down, refined, and elaborated from the original ten that Larry Speck and I wrote). The focus of the tasks was to contribute to effective resource management of the university's capital assets and future investments. The six revised tasks were as follows:

### 1. Historical Inventory and Preservation/Adaptive Re-Use Plan

A historical inventory and preservation/adaptive re-use plan will be a critical piece of an integrated planning process. The adaptive re-use potential of individual historic structures will be a significant driver of the overall plan. These efforts would identify the historically significant buildings and places on the University of Texas campus and would catalog the features that make them significant. The task will include a full survey of the building stock with evaluation as to which buildings are eligible for National Register designation. The Getty Foundation project surveyed the 40 acres [16 hectares] in terms of National Register eligibility, but the rest of the campus needs to be surveyed (UT Austin School of Architecture and Volz & Associates, 2011). . . .

### 2. Mobility Plan

Based on up-to-date existing conditions, data provided by the university team will develop an integrated campus-wide mobility plan that links pedestrian, bicycle, automobile, mass transit, and service vehicle circulation both to and from the campus and within the campus. This will require a thorough assessment of the current systems and a projection of loads and needs for the future. Particular emphasis will be placed on the proposed light-rail corridor that is projected to go through the campus on San Jacinto Boulevard and its impact on all systems of movement in this part of the city. . . .

## 3. Sustainability Plan

The focus of this first phase of sustainability planning is on reduction of energy and water consumption and on enhancing overall building performance. Planning for sustainable use of energy and water has the highest potential for a significant return on investment. A range of university growth targets will be identified by use type and building type to determine a baseline for current energy consumption. . . .

## 4. Space Management Assessment Tool

This task will focus on the development of a space management assessment tool that will provide analysis of existing space use and ongoing support for academic and facilities planning. Visualization of existing space use will be based on the metrics developed in the analysis phase and will be informed by existing and proposed academic plans. This tool will serve to integrate and visualize multiple data sources, to present opportunities for more cost-effective organization of university space, and to surface opportunities for more effective implementation of academic goals. . . .

## 5. Development Framework Plan

Formulation of a long-term development framework will allow the university to respond rapidly to its changing needs and opportunities. . . . In addition to addressing short-term priorities, the plan will provide a long-term vision for a distinctive, attractive, and memorable place. The framework will also allow the university to plan for the logical provision of infrastructure to meet future program growth.

*Campus Infill and Building Replacement*
This task will identify campus infill and building replacement opportunities. This plan will generate a set of sites where buildings could be added in a way that would enhance both open spaces and the operation of the campus while also providing for expansion. . . .

*Connectivity—Unification Plan*

The framework plan will address opportunities for knitting together various districts of the campus with a particular focus on the portion of campus to the east of San Jacinto Street/Waller Creek and on the portion of campus to the west of that divide. . . .

*Scenarios*

The analysis will provide a foundation for the evaluation and integration of currently proposed projects and plans as well as future options for growth and development. . . .

### 6. Design Guidelines for Buildings

Create new design guidelines for buildings on the campus and update the design guidelines from the Pelli plan as appropriate. This will include analysis of potential improvements in performance of existing buildings as well as footprints, massing, solar shading, and materials for new construction. Rather than a single set of hard rules for the entire approximately 350-acre [142-hectare] campus, a more flexible set of guidelines will be developed that can respond to the differences between the historic 40 acres [16 hectares] and the newer eastern side of the campus, as well as to differences in building types and construction budgets.

Clear goals remained in these tasks. The heart of the effort was the fifth task—the development framework plan. This measure was viewed as the first phase of a more comprehensive campus master plan that would encompass the other elements conceived by Speck and me. The other tasks would contribute to this development framework plan. Speck, Pat Clubb, and I devised a strategy to help President Powers and the other top UT Austin administrators (called the budget council) to move ahead with the first phase of the plan. We identified several pressing reasons, including the following:

- The university was facing serious safety issues relating to circulation in and around campus, i.e., conflicts between vehicles, pedestrians, and bikes.
- The university was facing internal connectivity challenges and fragmentation among different precincts.

- The City of Austin was undertaking major planning efforts which would affect the university, i.e., the upzoning of the West Campus neighborhood, the redevelopment of the Waller Creek corridor, the urban rail proposal, the downtown plan, and the city comprehensive plan.
- The State of Texas was rethinking the capital complex, which would probably impact the campus.
- Where would we put 10,000 more students and the associated faculty and staff?
- The quality of the campus landscape was being degraded by incremental decisions such as the location of signs, bicycle racks, food carts, and enlarged building footprints.

Although Pat Clubb believed in the value of Sasaki's space management assessment and planning tool, other administrators were not convinced and remained concerned about its cost ($675,000). Dr. Clubb was able to negotiate for a portion of the planning tool and a reduction of the overall cost to $1.3 million, which was approved by President Powers and the university's budget council in May 2011, and the planning process began that summer.[11] The Sasaki team was led by the low-key Daniel Kenney and the high-energy Philip Parsons.[12] To support the Sasaki team, we organized a leadership team (Pat Clubb, Steve Kraal, David Rea, Sharon Wood, Sam Wilson, and me), an advisory committee, and five task groups. Dr. Clubb and I cochaired the twenty-member advisory committee, which included the business and engineering school deans,[13] faculty members, two students, the associate director of athletics, and administrators. The task groups focused on historic resources, mobility, energy conservation, decision support tools, and sustainability. The president's sustainability steering committee served as the task group for sustainability. A key principle of the plan would be to link the university's mission with place-making.[14]

Larry Speck was invited to join the Sasaki team as a subconsultant, so a remnant of the architecture faculty–led team idea persisted. Speck is a sixth-generation Texan from Friendswood, a small town on the Gulf Coast. Educated at MIT, the Topaz Medallion recipient was the design leader of Page Southerland Page (now Page). As the former dean of the

School of Architecture and a member of the faculty building advisory committee, Larry had deep knowledge of the campus, which was reflected in the guidebook about campus architecture and planning that he had coauthored with Richard Cleary (Speck and Cleary 2011).

A university campus is a community. The campus plan would state what the University of Texas at Austin community wanted its campus to look like in the future. The goals were adjusted to budget constraints with the hope that a more comprehensive approach would occur as funding increased and the process illustrated a positive ROI.

## Fixin' to Plan

And so we got started on both the city and the campus plans, passing through the Texan "fixin'" or getting ready stage. Even as we began, challenges arose. In Austin, in spite of a commitment to extensive community involvement, a few key neighborhood leaders would agitate for even more participation (well, actually, control) throughout the process. They were skeptical about the potential for increased density and concerned about the perceived negative consequences more development might bring to their neighborhoods.

On campus, we would need to continue to make the case that the plan would produce a positive ROI. The term "framework" also became associated with the Framework for Excellence Action Plan developed by the UT System chancellor, Francisco Cigarroa. The chancellor's plan came on the heels of a heated public debate about the essence of the role of a leading research university in Texas. To avoid confusion, we called the Sasaki effort the "campus development plan" instead of the development framework plan. Meanwhile, after several years of discussion, the possibility of establishing a medical school at UT Austin began moving ahead. A new medical school clearly had significant spatial planning implications for the campus and would need to be addressed in the plan.

My kind of plan begins with setting goals that state where our leaders and constituents want to go. We did this in Austin and at UT. In Austin, the city council set broad goals and principles, and then more specific "objectives" (goals in my view) related to those principles. At the campus, tasks, which addressed university spatial planning goals, were refined and adjusted to the reality of the university budget. In both cases, a realization existed that the planning process would be a significant undertaking. From my perspective, the plans presented opportunities to apply my experience to the university where I worked and the city where I lived. As a result, I had a considerable stake in the outcomes.

# 2 — READING LANDSCAPES

## AN UNDERSTANDING OF HUMAN ECOLOGY

The strata of the Earth is a jumbled museum. Embedded
in the sediment is a text that contains limits and boundaries.
. . . In order to read the rocks we must become conscious
of geologic time, and the layers of prehistoric material that is
entombed in the Earth's crust.
— Robert Smithson

We ignore what lies below our feet at our own peril. Maps represent a wide variety of geographical phenomena. As John Hessler of the Library of Congress observed, "Most maps are about how we as a civilization, as different cultures, perceive our lives in this box that we live in" (quoted in Shapiro 2015). I enjoy reading and making maps, including those displaying the physical, biological, and social structures of places. I believe that maps can help us better understand our surroundings. As a result, the Imagine Austin comprehensive planning process initially disappointed me because so much time was devoted to talking about talking and relatively little to analyzing mapped information. Maps certainly were present at the many public meetings and workshops, but often more as backdrops than centerpieces for discussion.

Austin is well mapped. Geographic information systems (GIS) maps are available for almost every conceivable phenomenon and feature. In some ways, these GIS data formed something of an information cloud for the process that could be strategically accessed from time to time. Several members of the citizens' task force, such as the young geographer Jonathan Ogren, had strong GIS skills and would from time to time produce their own maps as well as make suggestions about how to improve the city's maps.

The city did provide a web-based community inventory, a large data-book about Austin. It included a broad range of information, with chapters devoted to the following topics:

- demographics and household trends,
- natural environment,
- land use and zoning,
- economic development and employment trends,
- housing and neighborhood conditions,
- transportation,
- public utilities,
- parks and recreation,
- community facilities,
- historic Austin, and
- urban design and urban form.

While introduced and mentioned at the beginning of the planning process, the community inventory remained largely in the background, in the cloud. Whereas these data played a supporting role in Imagine Austin, environmental information had been much more influential in Austin Tomorrow. This was a pity because Imagine Austin's database, especially the mapping, was considerably more comprehensive than its 1970s predecessor. In fact, Ian McHarg and his WMRT colleagues were pioneering natural systems mapping in projects like their Lake Austin plan (Wallace, McHarg, Roberts, and Todd 1976 [hereafter WMRT 1976]; Steiner 2011) that would become commonplace through the spread of GIS technologies.

In their planning projects during the 1960s and 1970s, WMRT collected paper maps, often at different scales. Different agencies follow their own specific mapping protocols, including the scales employed. For instance,

US Geological Survey topographic and geology maps differ significantly from those on soil types, erosion potential, and drainage patterns produced by the US Natural Resources Conservation Service (called the Soil Conservation Service in McHarg's day). The boundaries of maps seldom corresponded to a planning area. As a result, McHarg and his colleagues needed to redraw the maps at a common scale, tape the maps together to match the planning area boundary, and then trace key features by hand. When crucial information did not exist, McHarg's team would consult with leading local scientists to produce original maps. They used permanent markers to record information, for instance, rock formations, floodplains, soil types, and wildlife habitat. The maps could be overlaid manually to display opportunities and constraints for development and conservation, a technique that dated back at least to the Olmsted firm in the 1890s (see Steiner 2011). McHarg's innovation was to order the information through an ecological lens. The process was time-consuming and labor intensive. Now, thanks to GIS technology, this work can be accomplished by a few clicks with a mouse.

Furthermore, through GIS and other technologies, our society has witnessed a steady improvement in our ability "to access and monitor the environment, observe systems in great detail over long periods of time, compile and analyze the resulting data, and display findings with great sophistication" (Federal Geographic Data Committee 2012, 1).

## Nature's Design (Austin)

As Austin expanded in the early 1970s, its leaders initiated the Austin Tomorrow plan. A key influence on that process was Ian McHarg's *Lake Austin Growth Management Plan* (WMRT 1976), "one of the earliest examples of water quality planning in the United States" (Karvonen 2011, 52; see also Karvonen 2008). Although several others from WMRT were involved in the creation of the plan (most notably Michael Clarke), it is still identified locally as "the McHarg Plan." Local leaders have told me that the Philadelphia firm was retained because of McHarg, and the plan reflects the ecological planning principles put forth in his landmark book, *Design with Nature* (1969).

In 1974 the Austin City Council authorized the preparation of a plan for the 92-square-mile (238-square-kilometer) area including Lake Austin and the watersheds of its tributaries. Encompassing the western parts of the city and to the west of the then city limits, the planning area covered a live oak–dominated undulating terrain situated over the Edwards and Trinity Aquifers. Austin, then as now, was growing; in fact, it has doubled in population every twenty years since 1895. The Lake Austin area was clearly fated for new growth but also possessed significant environmental amenities. For example, the Edwards Aquifer, a vast limestone formation, is one of the world's most copious artesian aquifers and is home to several endemic species. According to McHarg and his colleagues, how and where growth "occurs will have a profound effect upon life and property and the Area's irreplaceable natural resources. The consequences of unplanned and uncontrolled growth will be felt not only by those persons living in the Lake Austin Area, but by a much larger population residing in the City of Austin and Travis County [the county where Austin is located] who will bear the costs of degraded environments and those actions required to deal with such conditions" (WMRT 1976, 2).

Such ideas were new for cities and counties in the early 1970s. The Clean Water Act had passed the US Congress in 1972,[1] and the nation had entered what became known as the "Environmental Decade." The momentum began with events such as the passage of the National Environmental Policy Act in 1969, signed into law on New Year's Day 1970 by President Richard Nixon, as well as the first Earth Day, then Earth Week, in April 1970. Published in 1969, *Design with Nature* provided one of the fundamental texts for this movement, and Austin's leaders wanted to put McHarg's ideas into action.

McHarg and his compatriots explicitly applied ecological understanding to their management plan. He advocated an "elastic organic plan" with "formal extensions." McHarg's focus was on planning infrastructure and protecting green spaces. The proper planning of infrastructure—water and sewer lines, roads and highways, and utilities—would help to guide new development to suitable locations and help to protect environmentally significant areas.

The Lake Austin plan consisted of a careful analysis of development trends, the determination of facilities and services necessary to accommodate that development, a detailed inventory of the natural environment with particular attention to the suitabilities for future growth, conservation and development principles, and suggested public policies to manage growth. Water quality received considerable attention in the WMRT plan, especially as it related to the sensitivity of the vast Edwards Aquifer as well as for other sources of Lake Austin. The water supplies were, and remain, important for fundamental domestic uses, wildlife habitat, and recreation.

McHarg's premise was that by studying the natural environment, one could identify certain possibilities for development as well as limitations. The constraints could prohibit some land uses while restricting others. This range of development opportunities and constraints corresponded with three proposed zones for the Lake Austin planning area: conservation, limited development, and development. The rules for each zone were founded upon a philosophy that land use and development controls should be as few in number and as uncomplicated as possible so that they may be effectively administered by a public agency and understood by the private sector (WMRT 1976, 49).

WMRT advocated elasticity, a flexibility guided by clear principles. McHarg contended that "natural regions" could be translated into "planning regions." As a result, he recognized the geodiversity of the Lake Austin planning area and defined four physiographic regions, tailoring the three zones (conservation, limited development, and development) for each region (figure 1). That is, the guidelines for the development zone in one region (for example, the Lake Austin Corridor Region) differed from the other three physiographic regions (e.g., the Plateau Region, the Hill Region, and the Terrace Region). Specific public policies were recommended for the planning area to guide future land use, open space, water supply, sewage collection and treatment, and highway construction and improvements.

The McHarg plan has had a varying influence in the Austin metropolitan region that continues to the present. Parts of the area covered by the plan were subsequently incorporated into other jurisdictions (West Lake Hills and Rollingwood). Both towns adopted several development and conservation standards, and as a result several suburban neighborhoods

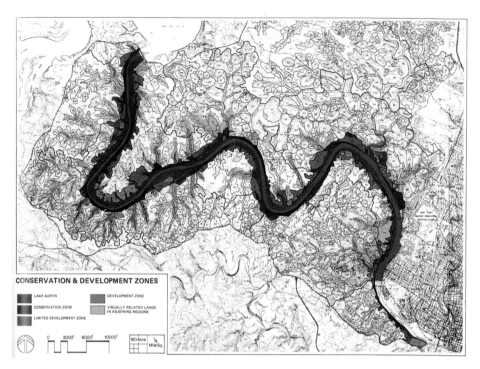

Figure 1. Conservation and development zones; from Ian L. McHarg Papers, Architectural Archives, University of Pennsylvania

in these jurisdictions as well as some inside the Austin city limits reflect many of McHarg's proposals. A former West Lake Hills city council member told me that the WMRT plan and *Design with Nature* provided "guiding lights for decades." Significant conservation areas, notably the eight-mile (12.9-kilometer) Barton Creek Greenbelt, were protected. I lived in an Austin neighborhood below magnificent live oaks that was influenced by McHarg's plan (figure 2). In other places, McHarg's vision was pursued less vigorously. Throughout the Austin metropolitan region, the Lake Austin plan continues to offer a basis for ongoing discussions and debates about environmental planning, water supplies, growth management, and smart growth policies.

The Lake Austin plan and McHarg's ideas contributed directly to Austin Tomorrow, which would have an even stronger and more lasting influence (see, for instance, Butler and Myers 1984; Swearingen 2010; Busch 2016).

Environmental quality formed a core basis for the plan, as is evident from its opening lines: "Each city possesses a spirit of its own—a reflection of the collective attitudes and aspirations of its citizens. The history of Austin shows that people here usually viewed their town on the Colorado River as a special district, a center of government, education, and community in a splendid environmental setting" (City of Austin 1980, 3).

Veteran city planner Dick Lillie led the process, and he was ardently supported by the mayor, city council, city manager, and planning commission. Andrew Busch describes Lillie as "a seasoned urban planner and liberal with roots in the democratic movements of the 1960s, versed in community organizing practices, and engaged with the emergent participatory planning literature" (Busch 2016, 92). Furthermore, Busch notes that Lillie was "a close associate of Roberta Crenshaw, founder of the Austin Environmental Council and the most vociferous opponent of the city's growth coalition" (ibid.). The plan itself is a delightful presentation of strong ideas and goals through good writing, thoughtful research, engaging drawings and photographs, and (pre-GIS) hand-drawn maps of

Figure 2. Steiner house, Austin, Texas; photograph by Frederick R. Steiner

exceptional clarity. The plan documents the city's social and environmental resources through prose and maps that support Austin Tomorrow's eight focus topics. Each topic was elaborated through goals, objectives, and policies. The eight topics (similar to elements) address urban design; economic development; environmental management; government and utility services; housing and neighborhoods; parks, open space, and leisure facilities; transportation systems; and health and human services.[2]

I will focus on the third topic, environmental management. For the Austin Tomorrow plan, "environmental management refers to the monitoring and regulation of society's impacts on natural physical elements" (City of Austin 1980, 33), or what we now call "ecosystem services" (Windhager et al. 2010). Economists and others have adopted the term "ecosystem services" to describe benefits that environments provide to humans at no monetary cost, benefits we would have to supply for ourselves if our surroundings ceased to provide them. Ecosystems regulate global and local climate; detoxify and cleanse air, soil, and water; regulate water supplies; control erosion and retain sediments; decompose, treat, and reuse waste; provide human health and well-being benefits; provide food; mitigate potential natural hazards; and provide cultural, educational, and aesthetic values (Windhager et al. 2010).

The 1979 Austin Tomorrow environmental management element included seven goals to discourage development in the areas of greatest environmental or agricultural value; assure the sensitivity of development to environmental features; protect and improve the water quality of Travis County's creeks, lakes, and aquifers; improve the management of solid waste; abate noise disturbances; reduce air pollution; and abate light pollution (City of Austin 1980). Natural resources were mapped in order to provide the knowledge to achieve these goals. The maps were used to determine development and preservation suitabilities across the city, the topic of the next chapter.

The 2009 community inventory prepared by the city planning staff for Imagine Austin included a detailed description of the natural environment, including land, water, climate, and habitat resources. The land resources of Austin and its extraterritorial jurisdiction (ETJ)[3] encompass five distinct geological regions: the Balcones Escarpment, the Edwards Plateau, the Rolling Prairie, the Blackland Prairie, and Colorado River terraces. The Balcones Escarpment is "a line of low hills extending through Central Texas and marks the break between the Great Plains and the Coastal Plains" (City of Austin 2009a, chap. 3, p. 1). To the west of the Balcones Escarpment, the Edwards Plateau Hill Country contains the karst aquifer with considerable groundwater. The Rolling Prairie "begins just east of the Balcones Escarpment and is a transition between the Hill Country of the Edwards Plateau and the Blackland Prairie of the Gulf Coastal Plain" (City of Austin 2009a, chap. 3, p. 4). The Blackland Prairie forms the western edge of the Gulf Coastal Plain. The Colorado River terraces follow the river, crossing the Balcones Escarpment into the Coastal Plain.

Each of these geological regions contains associated soils. The Blackland Prairie and the floodplains along the Colorado River and its tributaries have particularly deep and rich soils. The US Department of Agriculture has identified a significant amount of prime farmland in the Blackland Prairie and Colorado River terraces (City of Austin 2009a). But with rapid urbanization, the amount of farmland shrank by 35,981 acres (14,560 hectares), from 298,462 acres (120,783 hectares) to 262,481 acres (106,222 hectares), that is, by 56.5 square miles (90.9 square kilometers) or a 12 percent loss in five years (City of Austin 2009a).

The Austin metropolitan region has relatively abundant water resources, but these creeks, rivers, lakes, springs, and aquifers require wise use and management, especially with climate change affecting fluctuations in precipitation. The hydrologic "centerpiece" is Barton Springs, "which discharges an average of 27 million gallons (102,206,118 liters) of water a day from the Barton Springs segment of the Edwards Aquifer. The springs feed Barton Springs Pool, one of the most popular attractions in Central Texas" (City of Austin 2009a, chap. 3, p. 13).

The Colorado River and its tributaries have historically been prone to dangerous flooding. These floods are now carefully managed through a series of dams and watershed protection. Even though the hydrologic system is harnessed, flash flooding still occurs, often with damage to life and property, as illustrated by the events over the 2015 Memorial Day weekend and again on Halloween morning later that year. After years of drought, the floods were surprises, with some areas of central Texas receiving 9 to

13 inches (23 to 33 centimeters) of rain in four to six hours over the Memorial Day weekend; there were twenty-three deaths, and hundreds of others lost their homes. The subsequent Halloween morning flash flood killed another six people statewide and caused more property damage. Clearly watershed management is an important safety and economic issue in Texas. Central Texas watersheds contribute to and sustain Austin's creeks and lakes (City of Austin 2009a) (figures 3 and 4).

Development in the watersheds, which drain to the Barton Springs segment of the Edwards Aquifer, Lake Travis, and Lake Austin, has been regulated since the Austin Tomorrow plan. In 1997 the Austin City Council increased protection in these watersheds in its designated drinking water protection zone (see table with figure 3). All other watersheds fall into the desired development zone. An unintended social consequence is that wealthier neighborhoods on Austin's west side overlay the more bucolic protection zone, while historically poorer communities in East Austin are in the development zone. However, rich and poor alike benefit from good, clean drinking water. Continued urban growth and a serious drought that began in 2011 require careful planning to sustain water supplies from both ground and surface sources for future generations of Austin citizens. Texas, after all, is a land of drought suddenly interrupted by floods, a condition of extremes that climate change will likely exacerbate.

According to the community inventory report, "Austin has a humid, subtropical climate characterized by hot summers and mild winters . . . [with the heaviest precipitation] in the spring and fall, due to stalled cold fronts and tropical storms and hurricanes moving inland from the Gulf of Mexico" (City of Austin 2009a, chap. 3, p. 49). However, in recent years, Austin's mild climate has grown hotter while the amount of precipitation has generally declined (2015 was an exception to this trend). Global climate change is likely a major contributor to the overall warmer, dryer conditions. In response, the city council adopted the Austin Climate Protection Plan in 2007. This plan aims to make the city carbon-neutral by 2020 and builds on the city-owned utility's (Austin Energy) pioneering green-building programs, which began in 1982.[4]

In addition to lakes and springs, trees present the most evident element of Austin's environmental quality.[5] The community inventory report states:

Trees are the most visible component of natural vegetative systems, and they provide innumerable ecological, economic, and social benefits. Trees provide shade and reduce the retention of heat in urban areas, create and hold soil, slow stormwater runoff and dampen flooding, sequester carbon and purify the air, reduce the energy costs to cool buildings, provide habitat, create beauty and comfort, help shape and define physical spaces (even calming traffic), and raise property values. In a world where virtually all built infrastructure depreciates, trees increase in size and value over time. And trees are at the heart of the image and health of Austin, the literal and figurative core of the city's green image. (City of Austin 2009a, chap. 3, p. 11)

Austin rests on the ecotones of three bioregions, "each with their own tree and plant communities: the Edwards Plateau, the Blackland Prairie, and the Post Oak Savannah" (City of Austin 2009a, chap. 3, p. 11). However, with ever-increasing urban and suburban development, Austin is losing its tree canopy and other valued plant systems. As a result, the city maps and monitors its tree canopy (figure 5). In addition, many trees died in Texas and Austin as a result of the 2011 drought and wildfires.

The Edwards Plateau, the Blackland Prairies, and the Post Oak Savannah provide habitat for many animals, including important endangered species. The four springs that constitute Barton Springs are home to two such species: the endangered Barton Springs salamander (*Eurycea sosorum*) and the rare Austin blind salamander (*Eurycea waterlooensis*). Considerable efforts have been undertaken to protect these salamanders, which swim freely with Austinites in the Barton Springs Pool.

The Save Our Springs (SOS) Alliance played a key role in these protection efforts. The alliance emerged in the early 1990s from a loose coalition of citizens concerned about the negative consequences of development in the Barton Creek watershed for water quality generally and Barton Springs Pool specifically. The alliance was responsible for the SOS ordinance. Adopted by the city in 1992, the ordinance regulates development in the Barton Creek zone, which includes Barton Creek and other streams draining to or crossing the Edwards Aquifer recharge zone.

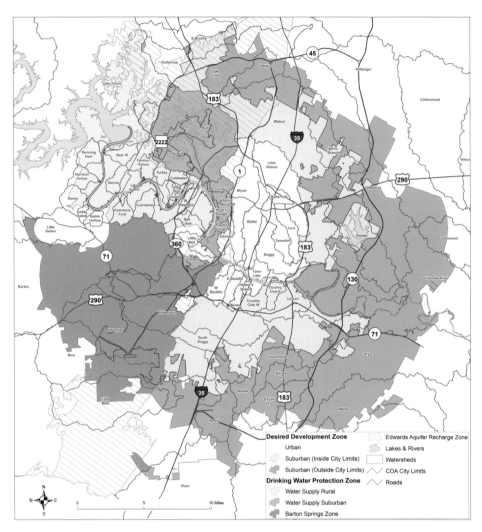

**Desired Development Zone**

Urban

Suburban (Inside City Limits)

Suburban (Outside City Limits)

**Drinking Water Protection Zone**

Water Supply Rural

Water Supply Suburban

Barton Springs Zone

Edwards Aquifer Recharge Zone

Lakes & Rivers

Watersheds

COA City Limits

Roads

0          5          10 Miles

Figure 3. City of Austin watershed regulation areas; courtesy of the City of Austin

## City of Austin Watershed Regulations Summary Table

| REGULATORY CATEGORY | ZONE | DESIRED DEVELOPMENT ZONE | | |
|---|---|---|---|---|
| | | Urban | Suburban City Limits | Suburban N. Edwards/ ETJ |
| **Impervious Cover** | **Uplands (Net Site Area)** | | | |
| | Single-Fam. | No Limitation | 50 – 60% | 45 – 60% |
| | Multi-Family | No Limitation | 60 – 70% | 60 – 65% |
| | Commercial | No Limitation | 80 – 90% | 65 – 70% |
| | **WQ Transition Zone** | N/A (No WQTZ in Urban) | 30% | 30% |
| | **Critical WQ Zone** | No IC except road crossings | No IC except limited road crossings | No IC except road crossings |
| | **Transfers Allowed** | No | Yes | Yes |
| **Waterway Classifications** | **Minor** | 64 acres | 320 – 640 acres | 320 – 640 acres |
| | **Intermediate** | 64 acres | 640 – 1280 acres | 640 – 1280 acres |
| | **Major** | 64 acres | over 1280 acres | over 1280 acres |
| **Waterway Setbacks** | **Critical Water Quality Zone** | | | |
| | Minor | 50 – 400 ft. | 50 – 100 ft. | 50 – 100 ft. |
| | Intermediate | 50 – 400 ft. | 100 – 200 ft. | 100 – 200 ft. |
| | Major | 50 – 400 ft. | 200 – 400 ft. | 200 – 400 ft. |
| | **Water Quality Transition Zone** | | | |
| | Minor | Not Required | 100 ft. | 100 ft. |
| | Intermediate | Not Required | 200 ft. | 200 ft. |
| | Major | Not Required | 300 ft. | 300 ft. |
| **Water Quality Controls** | **Treatment Standard** | Sedimentation/ Filtration | Sedimentation/ Filtration | Sedimentation/ Filtration |
| | **Alternatives Strategies Allowed** | Yes | Yes | Yes |
| | **Optional Payment-in-Lieu** | Yes | No | No |

| REGULATORY CATEGORY | ZONE | DRINKING WATER PROTECTION ZONE | | |
|---|---|---|---|---|
| | | Water Supply Suburban | Water Supply | Barton Springs |
| **Impervious Cover** | **Uplands (Net Site Area)** | | | R / BC / C * |
| | Single-Fam. | 30 – 40% | 1 unit per 1-2 ac. | 15% / 20% / 25% for all uses |
| | Multi-Family | 40 – 55% | 20 – 25% | |
| | Commercial | 40 – 55% | 20 – 25% | |
| | **WQ Transition Zone** | 18% | 1 SF unit / 3 acres | 1 SF unit / 3 acres None over recharge |
| | **Critical WQ Zone** | No IC except road crossings | No IC except road crossings | No IC except road crossings |
| | **Transfers Allowed** | Yes | Yes | No |
| **Waterway Classifications** | **Minor** | 128 – 320 acres | 64 – 320 acres | 64 – 320 acres** |
| | **Intermediate** | 320 – 640 acres | 320 – 640 acres | 320 – 640 acres |
| | **Major** | over 640 acres | over 640 acres | over 640 acres ** Williamson & Slaughter Creeks have 128 – 320 acre minor |
| **Waterway Setbacks** | **Critical Water Quality Zone** | | | |
| | Minor | 50 – 100 ft. | 50 – 100 ft. | 50 – 100 ft. |
| | Intermediate | 100 – 200 ft. | 100 – 200 ft. | 100 – 200 ft. |
| | Major | 200 – 400 ft. | 200 – 400 ft. | 200 – 400 ft. (Barton 400 ft. min.) |
| | **Water Quality Transition Zone** | | | |
| | Minor | 100 ft. | 100 ft. | 100 ft. |
| | Intermediate | 200 ft. | 200 ft. | 200 ft. |
| | Major | 300 ft. | 300 ft. | 300 ft. |
| **Water Quality Controls** | **Treatment Standard** | Sedimentation/ Filtration | Sedimentation/ Filtration | Non-Degradation |
| | **Alternatives Strategies Allowed** | Yes | Yes | No |
| | **Optional Payment-in-Lieu** | No | No | No |

* R = Recharge Zone; BC = Barton Creek Contributing; C = Other Contributing.
Other acronyms: ETJ = Extra-Territorial Jurisdiction; IC = Impervious Cover; SF = Single-Family Residential; WQ = Water Quality.

Figure 3, continued.

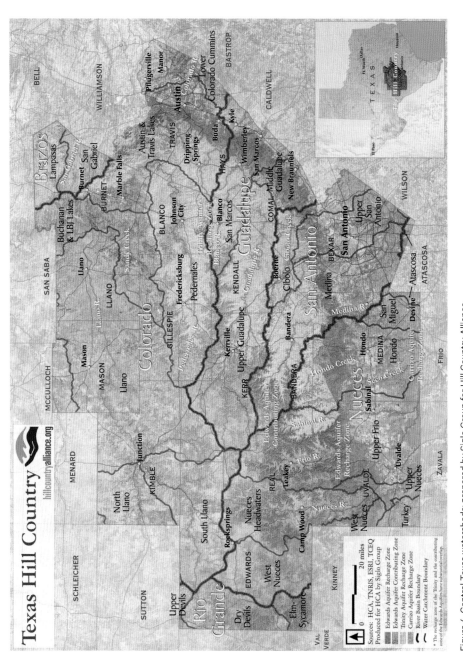

Figure 4. Central Texas watersheds; prepared by Siglo Group for Hill Country Alliance

In addition to the salamanders, the Balcones Escarpment is home to eight endangered species (two neotropical migratory songbirds and six karst invertebrates) plus another twenty-seven important species of concern for protection. To protect this habitat, local agencies cooperated with the federal government in 1996 to create a plan. The effort was led by the Austin School of Architecture environmental planning professor Kent Butler (now deceased). This innovative plan led to the creation of the Balcones Canyonlands Preserve and is widely acknowledged as a pioneer habitat conservation plan (Beatley 1994; Layzer 2008). Butler and his colleagues recognized that in order to protect specific species, their habitat needed to be preserved. This approach has been subsequently encouraged by the US Fish and Wildlife Service and other agencies.

The initial goal of the Balcones plan was to preserve a minimum of 30,428 acres (12,314 hectares) of land with important habitat for the golden-cheeked warbler (*Setophaga chrysoparia*) and the black-capped vireo (*Vireo atricapilla*) by 2016. In addition to preserving the habitat of these two endangered bird species, Austin and Travis County agreed to manage the population of two rare plants and sixty-two unique karst features known to be important for rare and endangered invertebrates. By 2012, all of the minimum goal of 30,438 acres (12,314 hectares) had been protected (Balcones Canyonlands Conservation Plan Coordinating Committee 2013). In addition, the city protects lands over the Barton Springs segment of the Edwards Aquifer through its Water Quality Protection Lands Program. In 2015 that program managed the protection of over 26,000 acres (over 10,522 hectares) through the purchase of land and conservation easements (figure 6).

The community inventory report did a reasonable job in documenting Austin's environmental resources and the efforts to manage those assets. Its authors also mapped out gaps in existing programs and challenges for the future such as climate change and air quality. However, the inventory could have been employed more creatively in the Imagine Austin process and its quality improved. Citizens' advisory task force member and GIS expert Jonathan Ogren in particular made many thoughtful suggestions on how to enhance the inventory. Some, but not all, of Ogren's recommendations were pursued. The opportunity was lost for advancing the state

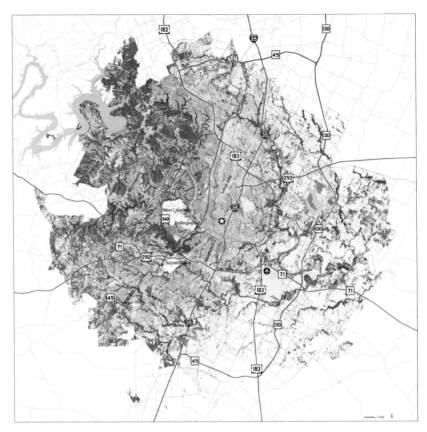

Figure 5. Tree canopy; courtesy of the City of Austin

of the art in mapping technologies and ecological thinking, as had been accomplished in Austin Tomorrow decades earlier.

Beyond the extensive environmental information, the community inventory report contained considerable socioeconomic data. The city's staff provided updates throughout the Imagine Austin process, most significantly after the 2010 US Census. Perhaps the most interesting fact revealed by the census was that East Austin had become much less segregated. African Americans in significant numbers had moved to the suburbs as parts of East Austin gentrified. Meanwhile, the Hispanic and Asian populations increased throughout the city to the point where Austin was a "majority-minority" city. The city's demographer, Ryan Robinson, briefed the task force and presented his "Top Ten Demographic Trends in Austin."[6]

According to my notes, his list included:

1. *No majority*. The City of Austin has now crossed the threshold of becoming a majority-minority city. Put another way, no ethnic or demographic group exists as a majority of Austin's population. The city's white share of total population dropped below 50 percent, probably during 2005, according to Robinson, and will probably stay there for the foreseeable future.

2. *Decreasing families-with-children share of the urban core population.* The share of all households within the city's urban core makeup of families with children is slowly declining. In 1970 the urban core's families-with-children share was just above 32 percent. The 2000 census puts the figure at not quite 14 percent. Moreover, with only a few neighborhood exceptions, the urban core is also becoming almost devoid of married-with-children households.

3. *African American share on the wane.* The city's African American share of total population will more than likely continue its shallow slide even as the absolute number of African Americans in the city continues to increase.

4. *Hispanic share of total population . . . will it ever surpass the white share?* Maybe not, but they'll be close to each other in just twenty-five years.

5. *Asian share skyrocketing.* The Asian share of total population in Austin almost doubled during the 1990s, leaping from 3.3 percent in 1990 to almost 5 percent by 2000, and stood somewhere near the 6.5 percent mark in 2010.

6. *Geography of African Americans, dispersion, and flight to the suburbs.* The critical mass and historically heavy concentration of African American households in East Austin began eroding during the 1980s, and by the mid-1990s had really begun to break apart. Over the past twenty-five years, middle-class African American households have left East Austin for the suburbs and other parts of Austin.

7. *Geography of Hispanics, intensifying urban barrios along with movement into rural areas.* Maps of Hispanic household concentrations from the 2000 census reveal the emergence of three overwhelmingly Hispanic population centers in Austin: lower East Austin (which also serves as

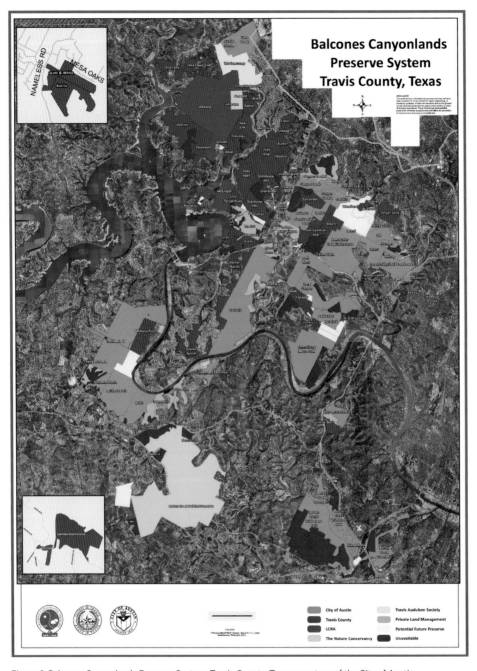

Figure 6. Balcones Canyonlands Preserve System, Travis County, Texas; courtesy of the City of Austin

the political bedrock of Austin's Hispanic community), greater Dove Springs, and the St. Johns area. Dove Springs shifted from being about 45 percent Hispanic in 1990 to almost 80 percent by 2000. St. Johns went from being 35 percent to 70 percent—this radical transition is clearly evident on the streets of St. Johns, a neighborhood that once hosted one of Austin's oldest African American communities.

8. *An increasingly sharp edge of affluence.* Maps of median family income from the 2000 census show an increasingly hard edge between affluent central Texas and less-than-affluent parts of the urban region. While some forms of residential segregation have decreased markedly over the past few decades in Austin, the degree of socioeconomic spatial separation has steeply increased. The center of wealth in Austin has slowly migrated into the hills west of the city.

9. *Regional indigent health care burden.* During the foreseeable future, the regional indigent health care burden will continue to grow and the city's disproportionate shouldering of the cost will increase as well.

10. *Intensifying urban sprawl.* The Austin region will continue to experience intense suburban sprawl. Although there was an enormous amount of residential development underway in 2010 within the urban core and in downtown Austin, the thousands of new units being created there will be only a drop in the regional bucket of total residential units created. There simply are very few land availability constraints in the territory surrounding Austin.

The cultural landscape of Austin has changed and become richer and more complex as it has become a majority-minority city within a considerably larger metropolitan region. The hilly, leafy metropolis remains a place of considerable beauty and a rich, yet fragile, natural environment.

## The Eyes of Texas: UT Austin Campus Planning (UT Austin)

Paul Cret prepared the most influential plan for the University of Texas campus in 1933. Cret was one of the most prominent architects in the United States from the first decade of the twentieth century through the 1930s. During the latter half of the twentieth century, his reputation waned with the rise of the International Style. The expatriate Germans from the Bauhaus opposed the Beaux-Arts tradition, and Paul Cret bore the standard for the French school in America.

Cret first entered the École des Beaux-Arts in his home city of Lyon, France. In 1896 he won the Prix de Paris, enabling him to study at the most important architectural school in the world at the time: the École des Beaux-Arts in Paris. He came to the United States in 1903 to teach at the University of Pennsylvania (McMichael 1983; also see Steiner 2011). Except for his service in the French army during the First World War, he lived in West Philadelphia until he dropped dead on a job site in 1945. While teaching classes and directing the architecture atelier at Penn, Cret maintained a robust practice in Philadelphia, designing such buildings as the Pan American Union in Washington, DC (1907–1917), the Indianapolis Public Library (1917), and the Detroit Institute of the Arts (1920–1927) (McMichael 1983; Laird 1990; Grossman 1996). In 1913 he prepared a plan for the University of Pennsylvania with his architecture students (Puckett and Lloyd 2015), which exhibited his growing interest in campus planning. The University of Texas plan was undertaken at the height of Cret's career.

Texans aim high, and early on they set their sights on a great state university. In fact, the 1876 state constitution mandated a university of the "first class."[7] Bolstered with oil revenue from state trust lands, a permanent university endowment fueled the construction of a physical plant worthy of these aspirations. The site of the original forty acres (sixteen hectares) of the University of Texas campus was chosen in 1881 after Austin won a popular vote over Galveston to be the location. The high spot of the city's edge became "College Hill," where construction of Old Main began in 1882. Plans by Cass Gilbert in 1909, James M. White in 1923, and Greene, La Roche and Dahl in 1928 contributed to the campus core, but it was the 1933 master plan by Paul Cret that "most significantly established the future design direction for the 40 acres and served as the model for the overall character of the University" (Cesar Pelli & Associates and Balmori Associates 1999, 11).

The University of Texas Board of Regents engaged Cret as consulting architect in March 1930, a post he retained until his death fifteen years later. In addition to his 1933 comprehensive development plan, the French American from Philadelphia participated in the design of nineteen campus buildings, as well as many terraces, retaining walls, and inner-campus roads (McMichael 1983). Of the previous plans and buildings, Cret's work exhibits the clear influence of Cass Gilbert, who had prepared a campus plan and designed the university's library (Battle Hall—figure 7) and education college (Sutton Hall). Battle Hall forms the keystone for the Gilbert-Cret spatial organization of the campus, framing the west side of what would become the Main Mall.

Cret's "Report Accompanying the General Plan of Development" contains attentive analyses of the existing buildings, previous plans (most notably those by Gilbert), and the hilltop, south-facing site (Cret 1933). The plan also presents a clear vision for the future (figure 8). His scheme respects precedent and context while charting a bold new course of action. Cret's work is deeply rooted in Beaux-Arts design principles.

Beyond the historicist façades, Beaux-Arts architects like Cret gave meticulous attention to the relationships among buildings. They organized these associations to build physical communities. Although to my knowledge Cret never used the word explicitly, this approach is "ecological," that is, concerned about the relationship of organisms (in this case, an "academic organism") with each other and with their environments.

Cret's plan consisted of large, carefully rendered watercolor plans and perspective drawings, as well as a written report (figure 9). His scheme sought to achieve an "elastic formal plan," derived from the writings about architecture as a "civic art" by Werner Hegemann and Elbert Peets (1922). Tulane University architecture historian Carol McMichael Reese explained this approach:

> Formality was achieved by grouping buildings around courts and
> arranging those groups about axes. Elasticity was achieved by "organic
> extensions" of existing and projected buildings and by the creation
> of secondary courts around the primary one at the center of the campus.
> The whole composition was guided by goals of "interrelation, balance,
> and symmetry." Interrelation was directed toward realizing elasticity;
> balance and symmetry, toward formality. (McMichael 1983, 84)

Cret's plan displayed considerable artistry and a deep appreciation of the role of beauty in creating a university of the first class. Linking plan making to implementation, Cret helped realize the ambitious vision through his participation in the design of many buildings on campus. He made generous use of Texas limestone in those buildings, connecting the halls of learning to the bedrock underlying most of the region.

Cret viewed his plan as flexible and adaptable, writing, "A general plan prepared today will have to be modified from time to time, to take account of changing conditions." He recognized, "To make an elastic formal plan is by no means an easy matter" (Cret 1933, 4).

Cret's plan pays careful attention to site conditions and the relationship of the campus to the city of Austin. Vistas, open spaces, the east-west orientation of the central campus (which made use of a ridge; the high point of College Hill became the site for the Main Building), sun angle and weather conditions, breezes, and topography contribute to the arrangement of buildings and circulation systems. Cret used live oak trees, which would grow to be large in stature, to frame the malls to the south, west,

Figure 7. Battle Hall, University of Texas at Austin, designed by Cass Gilbert, 1909–1910; photograph by Frederick R. Steiner

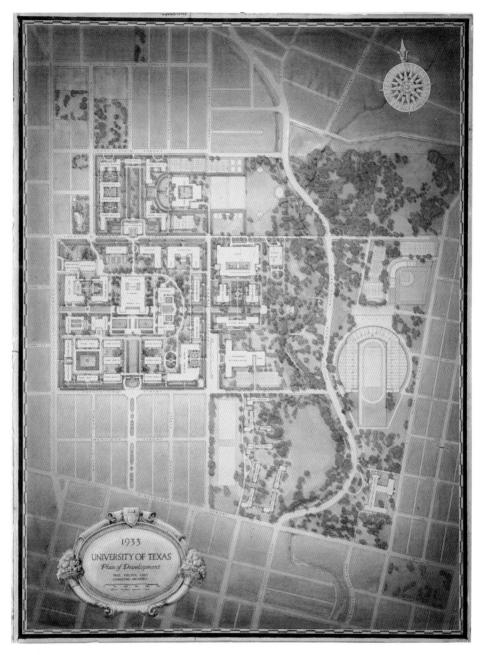

Figure 8. Paul Cret plan of the development for the University of Texas at Austin (1933);
Paul Philippe Cret Collection, © H2L2 Architects/Planners, Alexander Architectural
Archives, University of Texas Libraries, University of Texas at Austin

and east of the Main Building. The live oaks planted as a result of the Cret plan were *Quercus virginiana*, not the native *Quercus fusiformis* which they resemble. *Quercus virginiana* behave better in formal settings. Cret built on the efforts of Dr. William Battle, a constant champion of campus planning and architecture and the long-standing chair of the faculty building advisory committee, and of the university's comptroller, John W. Calhoun, who worked to preserve and expand trees on campus, especially live oaks.

As Speck and Cleary describe, "Besides the trees Calhoun planted, an enduring legacy of his passion is his inventory compiled in 1942, 'Trees of the Campus of The University of Texas,' that identifies every tree known to have preceded the founding of the University and all plantings since 1905. Cret received additional guidance from the Kansas City landscape architects Hare and Hare, whom the University had retained in 1932" (Speck and Cleary 2011, 31). Traffic flow between the university and the surrounding city is an important, recognized challenge. Because the Jeffersonian north-south, east-west grid of the campus is shifted from the original southwest to northeast grid of the city, the tenuousness of the connections is exacerbated.

Cret envisioned the stream, Waller Creek, running along the then east side of the campus, as an important opportunity to link the campus to the city. "This element of the campus," he wrote, "can be developed into a most attractive feature, without entailing large expenditures" (Cret 1933, 32).

One of the most noteworthy aspects of Cret's plan is its acknowledgment that change is inevitable. He presented careful provisions for growth. In particular, Cret recognized that sports would be an important driver of campus change. He observed, "The future of intercollegiate athletics, and especially of the exhibition games requiring very large accommodations for the public, is a subject of great controversy" (Cret 1933, 17).

Plans to expand the football stadium in 1969 generated "great controversy" indeed. The expansion plans encroached upon the Waller Creek corridor. Student activists chained themselves to trees and bulldozers, and the Austin environmental movement sprouted a new branch as the term "tree hugger" emerged. When the city expanded in the early 1970s, these environmental leaders initiated the Austin Tomorrow plan in response. The Cret plan continued to more or less guide development into

Figure 9. Paul Cret's watercolor perspective of the future development of the University of Texas at Austin (1933); Paul Philippe Cret Collection, © H2L2 Architects/Planners, Alexander Architectural Archives, University of Texas Libraries, University of Texas at Austin

the mid-twentieth century, but as the campus expanded to the east in the decades after World War II, the campus architecture moved further and further away from Cret's Mediterranean Beaux-Arts palette. During the late twentieth century, UT Austin detoured away from a strong cohesive architectural vision, and as Speck and Cleary note, campus planning of that era "revolves more around administrators than architects" (Speck and Cleary 2011, 37). The resulting modern structures of the late twentieth century have proved to be less popular on campus than the Cret and Gilbert predecessors.

Cesar Pelli & Associates, Balmori Associates, and Danze & Blood were responsible for the 1999 University of Texas at Austin master plan, which was undertaken in part to address concerns about the declining architectural character of the campus. The primary goal of the plan was to "support and embody a sense of community for students, faculty, and staff and to create a sense of place that will remain strong and clear in the memories of the graduates. Another objective is to reverse the current tendency toward decentralization of planning in response to growth. The new Master Plan . . . addresses the planned growth of an already mature campus" (Cesar Pelli & Associates and Balmori Associates 1999, 33).

The Pelli team conceived the plan with the philosophy that "responsibility for the future development of the University should be assumed only after understanding, respect and love of its past have been acknowledged, because it is in these earlier buildings and open spaces that we find the essence of our community. These buildings are flexible and enduring, and these open spaces encourage interaction and pedestrian comfort. They should be the model and inspiration for future development" (Cesar Pelli & Associates and Balmori Associates 1999, 28).

The 1999 campus master plan defined seven objectives and organizing principles:

1. To return the core campus to pedestrians and keep vehicular traffic to the edge of the campus
2. To use the architectural language of Paul Cret's original works as the point of departure for the design of new structures
3. To establish a community of landscaped open spaces, working in concert with buildings to extend and reknit the campus[8]
4. To add substantially to on-campus housing, thus creating a more complete academic community
5. To establish new centers of student activity, reinforcing housing and academic uses to enhance a full on-campus life
6. To concentrate future construction in the core campus rather than on the fringes
7. To enhance public perceptions of and access to the campus through strengthened identity and wayfinding programs (Cesar Pelli & Associates and Balmori Associates 1999, 33)

To pursue these objectives, the Pelli team relied on reading the architectural language created by Cret. Fred Clarke, a leading member of the Pelli team, had studied architecture at UT Austin and had intimate knowledge of Cret's creation. As a result, the Pelli plan advocated "A Return to the

Architectural Vocabulary of Paul Cret" (Cesar Pelli & Associates and Balmori Associates 1999, 43). Pelli, Clarke, and their colleagues noted that as UT Austin had expanded from the 1950s through the 1970s, "a number of structures were built in important locations without regard for the patterns and hierarchy of open spaces first defined in Paul Cret's 1933 master plan. Expediency took precedence over aesthetic qualities, and the important architectural attributes of siting, detail and material were ignored" (ibid.).

The Pelli plan proposed systems for the scale and massing of new building towers and roof forms, façade composition, entrances, and a material palette that evolved from the campus planners' inventory of similar elements created by Cret and the other designers who implemented his plan. Likewise, the Pelli team advocated an outdoors character that returned "to the Equilibrium between Building and Open Space" (Cesar Pelli & Associates and Balmori Associates 1999, p. 61). To move toward a more pedestrian campus, the plan's first objective, the Pelli team identified sites for new parking garages around the campus periphery.

Fred Clarke and his Pelli colleagues identified Waller Creek as a "beautiful gift, shaded by magnificent cypress, willow, live oak, pecan and elm trees; it is also the home of birds, squirrels and other wildlife" (Cesar Pelli & Associates and Balmori Associates 1999, 73). They suggested creating a richly vegetated glen around the stream. The transformation would result in a "restful and serene place" for studying and leisure.

The preservation of the historic campus core became the focus of a subsequent study. A good portion of the 2011 Getty Foundation–supported preservation study is devoted to reading the historic landscape of the forty acres. Its authors evaluated the historic resources of the campus core according to their eligibility for the National Register of Historic Places, beginning with the one currently listed building—Battle Hall. The plan includes both building and landscape features. The preservation planning team assessed the significance of the whole forty acres as well as seven subdistricts. They concluded:

> The University of Texas Forty Acres is a nationally-significant example of Beaux-Arts campus planning, one of the largest and most coherent in the country. . . . The plan of the campus is primarily the work of Cass Gilbert

and Paul Cret. Landscape architects Sidney J. Hare and S. Herbert Hare (respectively father and son), architect Herbert M. Greene and sculptor Pompeo Coppini each contributed works of high artistic value. The value of the campus design comes not merely from the individual contributions of these masters, but from the fact that they each joined in a collaboration that spanned many decades. (UT Austin School of Architecture and Volz & Associates 2011, 26)

## Culture's Design (UT Austin)

As with the city, an extensive GIS database existed for UT Austin as the Sasaki team members began their work. They made excellent use of the GIS database and augmented it with their own analytical maps of the 430-acre (174-hectare) campus. The Sasaki team used an interactive mandala to organize campus data, including maps (figure 10). Around the mandala, the overarching themes of campus quality, campus use, connectivity, and sustainability were arranged. Two additional rings were inside. The first ring included academic excellence, the student experience, capacity for growth, connectivity and access, the role in the city, campus ecology, resource management, traditions and identity, and landscape. The inner ring included the eight big transformative ideas for the campus (see next chapter for an explanation of these ideas).

Based on their experience at other major research universities and knowledge of past UT Austin trends, the members of the Sasaki team observed that the demand for new buildings would continue to grow even if enrollment remained stable. New buildings would be needed for research, especially interdisciplinary endeavors and new areas of exploration, as well as for student housing. The university offered a relatively small amount of on-campus housing, which the administration had long sought to increase. Among other reasons, on-campus living is believed to improve graduation rates. More new parking garages were needed to emphasize the dominance of pedestrians on campus. Based on historical trends and the expectation of a new medical school, Sasaki's team estimated that UT Austin could continue to grow by 2.4 million square feet (222,967 square meters), or roughly 10 percent, per decade (figures 11 and 12).

To identify the best locations for this projected growth, the Sasaki team divided the campus into three zones formed by natural and urban conditions (figure 13). The historic core of the campus consists of 196 acres (79.3 hectares). This zone was called "core" instead of "west" so as not to confuse it with the West Campus neighborhood outside the university. The city had upzoned that neighborhood in 2004, and it experienced considerable residential and commercial growth as a result. The central zone encompasses 182 acres (73.7 hectares), while the east zone contains 52 acres (21 hectares). Whereas the east zone (across an interstate freeway) was included in the inventory, detailed planning was not undertaken for it because of the limited scope of the first phase.

Conditions varied across these three zones, with impervious surface and building density covering 35 percent of the core, 23 percent of the central, and 19 percent of the east zones (figures 14 and 15). The floor area ratio (FAR) was accordingly also higher in the core than in the central and east zones (figure 16).[9]

These densities and existing tree cover (figure 17) affect outdoor comfort (figure 18). In addition, large asphalt parking areas in the central and east zones increase the ambient temperature, creating inhospitable outdoor experiences, especially in the summer, and raising the financial and environmental costs. The financial costs relate to the increased expenses for air conditioning, while environmental impacts include increased storm water runoff and heat islands. The rapid runoff of storm water contributes to flash flooding. Vast parking lots add to nonpoint pollution as well as warmer temperatures. These environmental factors provided another reason to build new parking garages.

Most of the campus drains into Waller Creek (figure 19). The stream corridor has been treated poorly by campus development in spite of Paul Cret's plan, which proposed the creation of a generous, informal park along the creek, an idea reinforced in the Pelli plan. During the twentieth century, development steadily encroached on the floodplain, leaving only a narrow, densely developed, and compromised corridor. The Sasaki team noted that while the flow of the stream is continuous and day-lighted through campus, many stretches are inaccessible. Currently, Waller Creek forms a barrier between the core and central campus zones. However,

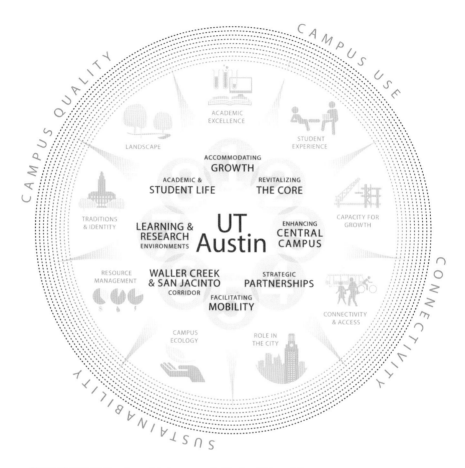

Figure 10. Organizational mandala; image created by Sasaki Associates,
© University of Texas at Austin

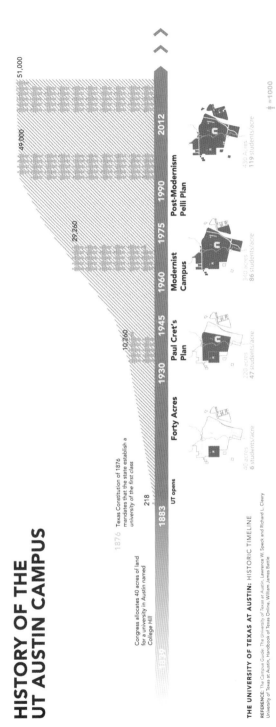

# HISTORY OF THE UT AUSTIN CAMPUS

THE UNIVERSITY OF TEXAS AT AUSTIN: HISTORIC TIMELINE

1836

1876 Texas Constitution of 1876 mandates that the state establish a university of the first class

Congress allocates 40 acres of land for a university in Austin named College Hill

218

| 1883 | Forty Acres | 1930 | Paul Cret's Plan | 1945 | Modernist Campus | 1960 | 1975 | Post-Modernism Pelli Plan | 1990 | 2012 |

UT opens

10,260

29,260

49,000

51,000

40 acres
6 students/acre

220 acres
47 students/acre

340 acres
86 students/acre

430 Acres
119 students/acre

= 1000

REFERENCE: The Campus Guide: The University of Texas at Austin, Lawrence W. Speck and Richard L. Cleary
University of Texas at Austin, Handbook of Texas Online, William James Battle

Figure 11. Historical timeline; image created by Sasaki Associates, © University of Texas at Austin

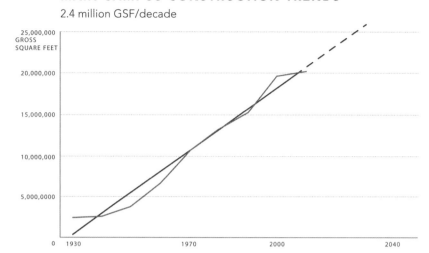

## MAIN CAMPUS CONSTRUCTION TRENDS
2.4 million GSF/decade

Figure 12. Main campus construction trends; image created by Sasaki Associates, © University of Texas at Austin

the corridor presents opportunities, as it contains several large trees and clumps of rich riparian vegetation.

Professor Ted Gordon, chair of UT's African and African Diaspora Studies Department and a member of the campus plan advisory committee, indicated an aspect of the cultural legacy of campus not addressed in the Pelli plan. With others, he found the placement of four Confederate "heroes" on the Main Mall and the South Mall offensive. The nine-foot-tall (2.7-meter), 1,200-pound (544-kilogram) bronze likeness of Jefferson Davis sat atop the steps of the Main Mall, where it had looked south toward the towering State Capitol since 1933. Statues of three other Confederates—General Robert E. Lee, General Albert Sidney Johnston, and Postmaster General John H. Reagan—are located below the live oaks of the South Mall (also called the South Lawn).[10] The location of more recent statues attempted to mitigate this history by recognizing Martin Luther King Jr. on the East Mall, pointing east to the Lyndon Baines Johnson Library and LBJ School of Public Policy, and Barbara Jordan looking north.

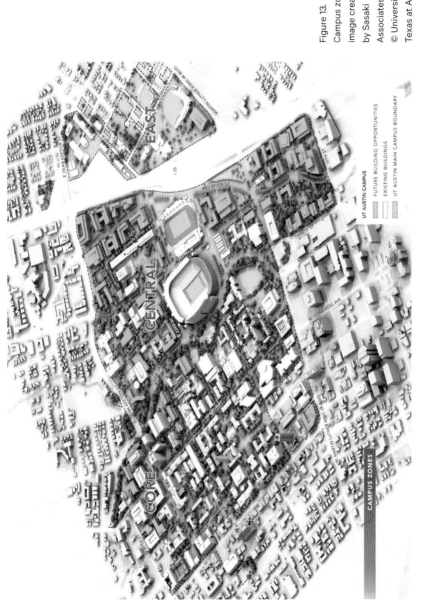

Figure 13. Campus zones; image created by Sasaki Associates, © University of Texas at Austin

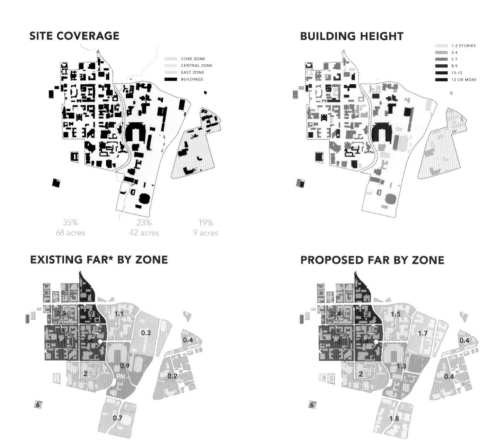

**SITE COVERAGE**

CORE ZONE
CENTRAL ZONE
EAST ZONE
BUILDINGS

35%        23%        19%
68 acres   42 acres   9 acres

**BUILDING HEIGHT**

1-2 STORIES
3-4
5-7
8-9
10-12
12 OR MORE

**EXISTING FAR* BY ZONE**

2.3    9    1.1
            0.3
              0.4
2
   0.9
      0.2
6
   0.7

**PROPOSED FAR BY ZONE**

2.4    2    1.5
              1.7
                0.4
2    1.3
        0.4
6
   1.8

Figure 14. Site coverage; image created by Sasaki Associates, © University of Texas at Austin

## SITE COVERAGE

CORE CAMPUS
CENTRAL CAMPUS
EAST CAMPUS
BUILDINGS

35%      23%              19%
68 acres  42 acres        9 acres

The Core Campus has a finer grain and higher density of building coverage relative to the other campus zones.

Land coverage varies significantly in the three zones. On the Core Campus, 35% of the land is covered by buildings. This number drops to 23% on the Central Campus and to only 19% on the East Campus.

## BUILDING HEIGHT

1-2 STORIES
3-4
5-7
8-9
10-12
12 OR MORE

The Core Campus has more tall buildings and a higher building density than the other campus zones.

Figure 15. Building density; image created by Sasaki Associates, © University of Texas at Austin

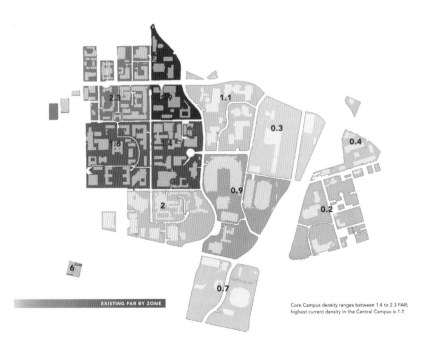

EXISTING FAR BY ZONE

Core Campus density ranges between 1.4 to 2.3 FAR; highest current density in the Central Campus is 1.1

Figure 16. Existing floor area ratio by zone; image created by Sasaki Associates,
© University of Texas at Austin

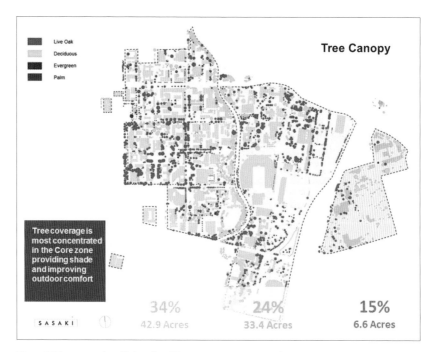

Figure 17. Tree cover; from University of Texas at Austin 2014 Landscape Master Plan
and Design Guidelines

(The placement of the César Chávez statue on the West Mall, also oriented
to the north, seems to have no geographical symbolism.) Still, the four
Rebels remained.

In addition, the Littlefield Fountain, which anchors the South Mall,
included an inscription that honored the Confederacy without mention-
ing slavery: "To the men and women of the Confederacy who fought with
valor and suffered with fortitude that states' rights be maintained." Major
George Washington Littlefield, namesake of the fountain, was a veteran
of the Eighth Texas Cavalry, popularly known as Terry's Texas Rangers.[11]
Littlefield fostered the fiction that the Confederacy existed for the "no-
ble" cause of "states' rights" somehow independent from maintaining the
"right" to enslave black people.

Littlefield was also responsible for the Confederate statues. He conceived a giant arch forming the south entry to the campus adorned with
the statues of Davis, Lee, Johnston, and Reagan. Littlefield enlisted the San

Antonio sculptor Pompeo Coppini to make the arch and statues. Coppini suggested a fountain instead of an arch and "a monument of reconciliation portraying World War I as the catalyst that inspired Americans to put aside differences lingering from the Civil War" (Speck and Cleary 2011, 88). Southern-born Woodrow Wilson, who had been president during World War I, and James Stephen Hogg, "the first native-born governor of Texas and an ardent supporter of the university," were added to the Rebels (ibid.).[12] The Wilson statue would eventually sit on the Main Mall parallel to Davis; Hogg would be located under the live oaks on the South Lawn with the three Confederates.

When Cret became the campus architect, he found "the composition of the monument incompatible with his design for the South Mall" (Speck and Cleary 2011, 88). As a result, and apparently to the displeasure of

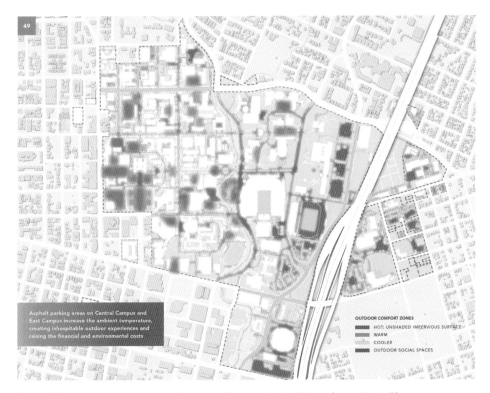

Asphalt parking areas on Central Campus and East Campus increase the ambient temperature, creating inhospitable outdoor experiences and raising the financial and environmental costs

OUTDOOR COMFORT ZONES

HOT: UNSHADED IMPERVIOUS SURFACE
WARM
COOLER
OUTDOOR SOCIAL SPACES

Figure 18. Outdoor comfort zones; from University of Texas at Austin 2014 Landscape Master Plan and Design Guidelines

Figure 19. Waller Creek; image courtesy of Michael Van Valkenburgh Associates and Waller Creek Conservancy

Coppini, Cret, a decorated World War I veteran himself, rearranged the statues to their current locations. Subsequently, in 1955 the Daughters of the American Revolution funded the statue of George Washington on the mall, which was also made by Coppini.

Although they certainly offended African Americans and some others, until recently, thousands of people have walked by the fountain and the statues without being repulsed or, perhaps more disturbing, without even giving the symbols a second thought. Dr. Gordon suggested that the space be reinterpreted to tell the story of slavery in the United States.

In the spring of 2015, candidates for president and vice president of the student government ran on a platform that included the removal of the Jefferson Davis statue, calling it "racism on a pedestal." They won, and, as we will see later, the student leaders would affect the statue's future.

## Urban Nature and Human Design

My kind of plan is grounded in reading landscapes and employing ecology, including human ecology, in that understanding. Ideally, a city plan should provide a more thorough analysis of the biophysical environment than Imagine Austin accomplished. This is possible, even necessary, for urban areas.

In 1984 McHarg protégés published two prescient books on urban ecological design: Anne Whiston Spirn's *The Granite Garden* and Michael Hough's *City Form and Natural Process*. They sought to illustrate explicitly how McHarg's ecological ideas are relevant to urban places. In these pioneering urban ecology texts, Spirn and Hough lay out the value of air, earth, water, plants, and animals and also bring them together as ecosystems. Our knowledge about urban ecology has expanded significantly since the 1980s (see Pickett et al. 2011; Grove et al. 2015).

We continue to sort out the place of nature in the city (see Steiner et al. 2016). As Pope Francis observed, "We are part of nature, included in it and thus in constant interaction with it" (Pope Francis 2015, 139). Instead of nature ending, as some contend (McKibben 1989), I believe our view of the natural world is expanding. Thus, we need to conceive a new urban nature, one where our actions restore and celebrate the world around us. We need to plan and design buildings and landscapes that give back to ecosystems, which are regenerative. A starting place is understanding what is suitable and what is not.

# 3 — DETERMINING SUITABILITIES

## A DISCOVERY OF OPPORTUNITIES AND CONSTRAINTS

Design depends largely on constraints.
— Charles Eames

Suitability analysis involves understanding the opportunities for change that a landscape presents, as well as its constraints. Ian McHarg advanced the art of suitability analysis with hand-drawn, and eventually computer-generated, maps of climate, geology, groundwater hydrology, surface water hydrology, topography, soils, vegetation, wildlife, and historical and current land use. GIS technology helped significantly to refine, develop, and advance such analyses. In addition to improving map accuracy, GIS facilitates the comparison of different mapped phenomena, that is, layers of spatial data. GIS also enables placing values and weights on specific mapped phenomena. For instance, soil types can be ranked for values such as productivity, erosion, and drainage.

The suitability analysis process works in the following way: a land use is suggested, say, agriculture or single-family housing. For agriculture, opportunities would include fertile soils, flat land, good drainage, a favorable microclimate, and relatively few existing trees and other plants. Constraints might include erodible and poorly drained soils, steep slopes, a high water table, and valuable wildlife habitat. Hazardous areas are also considered constraints, such as places prone to flooding, wildfires, or landslides. For single-family housing, the opportunities and constraints would be much the same. The history of the site could present additional challenges for housing development, as could earthquake and storm-surge hazards. So, many parcels of land are equally good for more than one use: farming and housing, for instance. Very early in my career, I recall visiting a site for a planned new community and hearing my boss, a crusty Harvard-educated landscape architect, say, "Look at where the farmers are growing the corn—that's the best place to put houses," as we gazed across the Ohio countryside.

In fact, Ohio farmers do practice a crop rotation of corn, soy beans, and tract houses. Plans should help sort out and rank competing possibilities: corn or houses, park or factory, Taco Bell or library. Real estate attorneys, developers, and land economists use the "highest and best use" concept when referring to a parcel of land based on a subjective view of local markets. McHarg took a more comprehensive perspective, asserting that an objective analysis of environmental, social, and economic factors would reveal the "intrinsic suitabilities" of land. If we seek to achieve more sustainable communities, we need to move past shorter-term highest and best uses and instead reinforce the more lasting intrinsic capabilities of places.

### Greenprinting (Austin)

The 1979 Austin Tomorrow plan contained development suitability factors for both the natural and urban environments. The authors of the plan explained their approach as follows: "Environmental indicators are mapped to show the location of environmentally fragile land[;] the procedure also reveals the most suitable locations for Austin's future growth" (City of Austin 1980, 109). The planners included a critique of the suburbanization process, pinpointing its deleterious consequences for both the natural and human urban environments. They also explained how continued suburban growth would increase the costs for city facilities and services.

McHarg's Lake Austin plan provided the environmental mapping prototype for Austin Tomorrow. Six maps were produced for the natural environment: (1) slopes, (2) geology, (3) prime farmland soils, (4) floodplains, (5) soils with septic tank limitations, and (6) synthesis. The synthesis map illustrated where there were no, one, two, or three environmental limitations (figure 20).

Austin Tomorrow also considered development suitability factors for the urban environment, a key innovation of this 1979 comprehensive plan. The planners used traditional land-use categories: residential neighborhoods, commercial and industrial districts, parks, greenbelts, and historic structures. Suitability for the urban environment involved protecting residential neighborhoods from increased traffic, incompatible land uses, and noise and glare while preserving water quality and waterway environments.

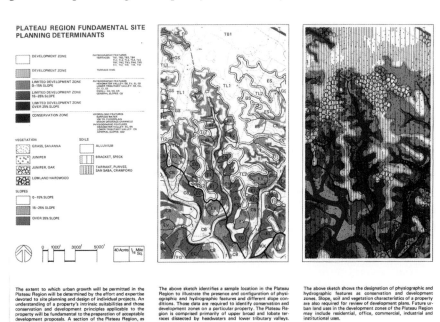

The extent to which urban growth will be permitted in the Plateau Region will be determined by the effort and expertise devoted to site planning and design of individual projects. An understanding of a property's intrinsic suitabilities and those conservation and development principles applicable to the property will be fundamental to the preparation of acceptable development proposals. A section of the Plateau Region, as shown on the accompanying sketches, illustrates the minimum information required to review development proposals for a particular property.

The above sketch identifies a sample location in the Plateau Region to illustrate the presence and configuration of physiographic and hydrographic features and different slope conditions. Those data are required to identify conservation and development zones on a particular property. The Plateau Region is comprised primarily of upper broad and lobate terraces dissected by headwaters and lower tributary valleys.

The above sketch shows the designation of physiographic and hydrographic features as conservation and development zones. Slope, soil and vegetation characteristics of a property are also required for review of development plans. Future urban land uses in the development zones of the Plateau Region may include residential, office, commercial, industrial and institutional uses.

Figure 20. Plateau region, fundamental site planning determinants; Ian L. McHarg Papers, Architectural Archives, University of Pennsylvania

Through the years, the city and its metropolitan region continued to grow. The SOS ordinance helped protect some areas in the west, but conflicts between development and environmental interests continued. Neighborhood organizations flourished and became more effective at stopping projects. The region sprawled and became more fragmented and congested. When an ambitious light-rail proposal was narrowly defeated in the 2000 election, civic leaders across the five metropolitan counties formed Envision Central Texas (ECT) in 2001. ECT developed a vision for the region and advocated that local government pursue and adapt that regional perspective.

The nonprofit organization ECT partnered with the Trust for Public Land (TPL) and the Capital Area Council of Governments (CAPCOG) to produce a "greenprint" for the Austin metropolitan area. According to TPL, greenprinting is a GIS model that "helps local governments and communities make informed decisions about conservation priorities" (Trust for Public Land 2005–2006, 5). The model consists of four steps:

1. data are collected that reflect community goals, [and] then
2. data are translated into GIS models,
3. criteria are weighted (valued) according to community goals, and finally
4. overview maps, parcel priority rankings, and reports are created. (Trust for Public Land 2005–2006, 5)

TPL and ECT conducted a greenprint for Travis County in 2005–2006, cooperating with the county, the City of Austin, and the UT Austin School of Architecture. We worked with many interested parties in the region.[1] Four criteria classes were identified for the model. The water quality/quantity class was composed of ten GIS map layers; the recreational class, of ten layers; the sensitive/rare environmental features class, of eight layers; and the cultural resources class, of five layers. Each of these four classes was weighted equally to produce the Travis County greenprint (Trust for Public Land 2005–2006) (figure 21).

After completing the Travis County greenprint, TPL and ECT joined with CAPCOG to produce greenprints for three additional metropolitan counties: Bastrop, Caldwell, and Hays. The greenprint team worked from

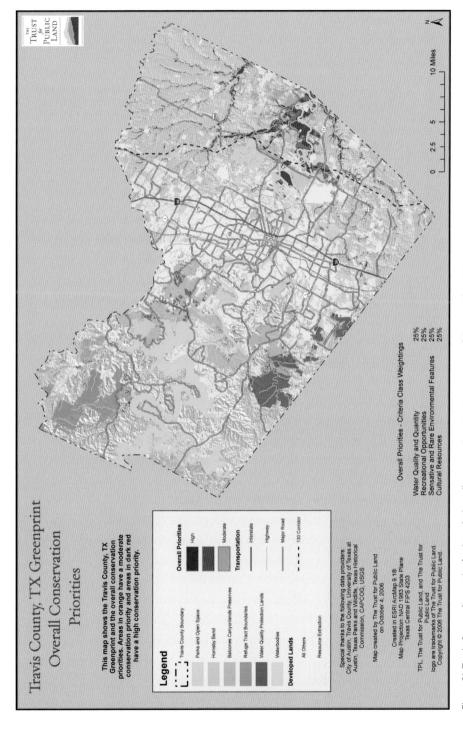

Figure 21. Travis County Greenprint for Growth: Overall conservation priorities; courtesy of the Trust for Public Land

May 2008 to October 2009 to tailor the model to fit the specific local conditions and priorities of each county. Six goals were established for the Central Texas greenprint:

- Protect Water Quality and Quantity
- Protect Sensitive Ecological Areas
- Preserve Farms and Ranch Land
- Enhance Recreational Opportunities
- Protect Cultural Resources and Historic Sites
- Protect Scenic Corridors and Viewsheds (Trust for Public Land 2009)

GIS maps were produced for each of these goals for the counties. The process resulted in a map of the regional overall conservation opportunities (figure 22). Although Imagine Austin did not produce suitability maps as Austin Tomorrow had, the greenprint maps fulfilled a similar role as the development suitability analysis for the natural environment in the earlier plan.

Imagine Austin also built on other ECT ideas for its preferred growth scenario, principally the "centers concept." This approach was integral to ECT's 2004 preferred vision for the region. The centers concept is grounded in the theory of transit-oriented development that has been advanced by Peter Calthorpe (1993), one of the two principal ECT consultants (the other was John Fregonese). Through the centers concept, "funding is targeted to expand the region's public system (including buses and rail), to implement a network of high capacity roadway lanes, and to build new arterials serving the mixed use centers" (Paterson and Mueller 2013).

The idea is to concentrate growth in specific areas for economic, social, and environmental benefits. This approach was affirmed through an extensive public outreach and response process. The concept was subsequently incorporated into the Capital Area Metropolitan Planning Organization (CAMPO) official 2035 regional mobility plan adopted in 2005. Sarah Eckhardt, a county commissioner who later became a county judge, led the effort to include activity centers in the CAMPO plan. Kirk Watson, a state senator and former Austin mayor, organized a transit working group in 2007–2009 that also supported and advanced the centers concept.[2] As a result, the CAMPO board voted to implement a 50 percent

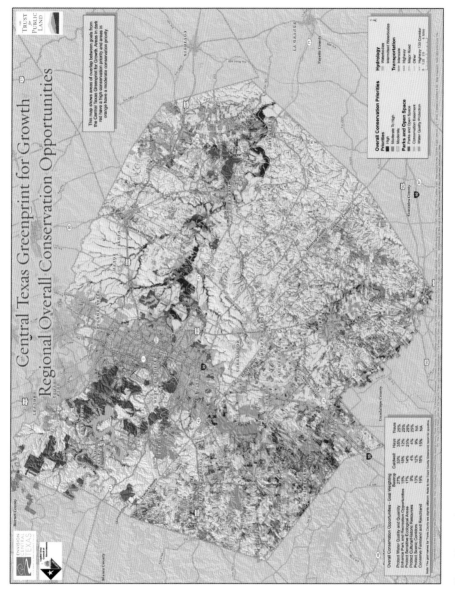

Figure 22. Central Texas Greenprint for Growth: Regional overall conservation opportunities; courtesy of the Trust for Public Land

"centers set-aside" for federal transportation dollars to help seed multiuse, multimodal population nodes throughout the region.[3]

The centers concept has a relatively long lineage in American planning. Robert Yaro of the Regional Plan Association (RPA) and the University of Pennsylvania links it to metropolitanism. According to Yaro, metropolitanism involves "promoting growth in a series of centers within a region and protecting environmental systems within growth boundaries of urban and suburban development" (Yaro 2012, 154). Yaro and his RPA colleagues employed the centers concept in their third regional plan, which connected a new network of suburban centers through a regional rail system (Yaro and Hiss 1996).

In Imagine Austin, centers formed part of the growth concept continuum that ranged in population and job growth size as well as development character. Specifically, the plan included regional centers (25,000–45,000 new people; 5,000–25,000 new jobs), town centers (10,000–30,000 new people; 5,000–20,000 new jobs), neighborhood centers (5,000–10,000 new people; 2,500–7,500 new jobs), mixed-use corridors, job centers, open space, high-capacity transit and transit stops, highways and other streets, redevelopment over the Edwards Aquifer, and other development within the city limits as well as outside them in the ETJ.

The possible economic, social, and environmental benefits of the centers concept are robust. The idea is fiscally conservative because investments in infrastructure and services are clustered. Less public funding is expended for construction and maintenance. Long-term services such as police, fire, teaching, water, and sewer costs can be reduced as well. Economic benefits extend to the private sectors because the concept provides stability to developers and other businesses for their investment planning.

In addition to the economic and fiscal benefits, the centers concept can result in positive environmental amenities. For instance, energy costs are reduced and water is conserved when more wildlife habitat and open space can be protected. By concentrating development, more prime farm and ranch lands as well as wildlife habitat can be preserved and commuting times are reduced. In addition, public health and built environment researchers observe that schools in walkable communities help reduce childhood obesity and asthma (see, for example, Rahman et al. 2011). The centers concept helps promote such walkable neighborhoods.

The draft Imagine Austin plan was released to the public on October 1, 2011, with the centers concept providing a cornerstone to its draft growth scenario. The idea behind scenarios is to provide stories for the future of a place. As medical doctors produce postmortems, these storylines present opportunities for planners to conduct "premortems" of the consequences of various actions. Imagine Austin anchored its story of the future largely around concentrating growth in centers.

The draft plan also directly and candidly posed the six major challenges and opportunities Austin faced in order to sustain its quality of life. First, while Austin is a great place to live, the city needs to preserve the attributes that contribute to its livability: "natural resources and recreational opportunities, friendly neighborhoods, a robust economy, and a thriving arts scene" (City of Austin 2011, 4). Second, cars and trucks congest city streets, and transportation choices need to be expanded. The plan encouraged more transit, bicycling, and walking opportunities. Third, the city was divided by race through planning and zoning until such divisions became illegal. Imagine Austin sought to address head-on the sins of past plans by closing "opportunity gaps" (City of Austin 2011, 5).

Fourth, in building on a more positive legacy of a past plan (specifically Austin Tomorrow), Imagine Austin advocated that trails and greenbelts, lakes and rivers, and parks and natural lands be considered a "core part of what makes Austin special" (City of Austin 2011, 5). Fifth, Imagine Austin promoted prosperity for all with an emphasis on "high-tech strengths, colleges and universities, youth culture, attractiveness to the 'creative class,' support for local independent businesses, and [a] unique music and arts community" (ibid.). Finally, the plan reinforced the need to collaborate regionally on issues "such as transportation, water resources, development of the region, environmental protection, climate change, and economic prosperity" (ibid.).

## Where to Grow: The Growth Concept Map (Austin)

The draft plan included a "growth concept" map that identified places for the city to expand, as well as future open space areas (figure 23). Growth areas were based on the centers concept, while new open space opportunities were derived in part from the greenprint. In addition to protecting

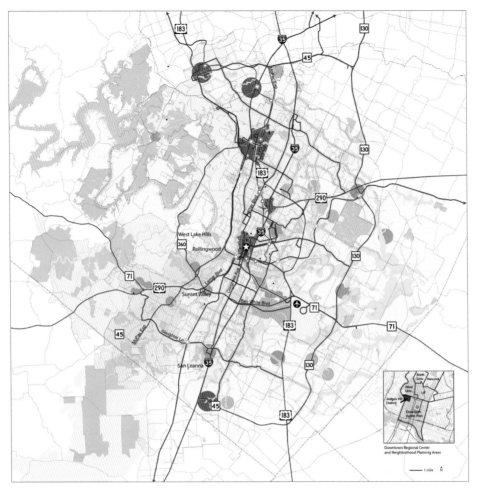

Figure 23. Growth concept map; courtesy of the City of Austin

aquifer and watershed lands to the west, the plan identified considerable new opportunities for parks and open space to the east, especially in flood-plains and areas with prime agricultural lands. The new open space areas in the eastern parts of the city would help balance past inequalities. Areas for new parks were also identified in the growing northern and southern parts of Austin and the ETJ. The growth centers were generally located away from environmentally sensitive lands and linked to a transportation system that included highways and high-capacity transit.

The growth concept map reflects suitable areas for development and conservation. The map was produced by planners using GIS to overlay social and environmental information. It reflects physical as well as political suitabilities and sensitivities.

## Big Ideas (UT Austin)

On March 21, 2012, David Rea, Larry Speck, and I met with the Sasaki team in their Watertown, Massachusetts, headquarters. At that point, the Sasaki team had accumulated considerable information about the campus. Our two-day charrette focused on how to present those findings to the advisory committee, task groups, and university administration. The initial thought was to organize the presentation around the theme of sustainability. Instead, we determined to focus on eight big transformative ideas with sustainability integrated throughout. Each of these opportunities would require major decisions and actions, and all of them are interdependent. Not all the "big ideas" would be addressed in the first phase of the plan, but the groundwork would need to be laid for necessary future planning. We explained the ideas as summarized here:

1. Accommodate Growth

   Research universities today are widely recognized as the catalysts for economic and social transformation in their regions. In fulfilling this catalytic role, research universities need to continue to grow. Growth at UT is essential to accomplishing university goals. . . .

2. Revitalize the Core Campus

   The Core Campus, bounded by Guadalupe Street, San Jacinto Boulevard, Martin Luther King Jr. Boulevard, and 27th Street, and including the original forty acres, contains the majority of UT's historic buildings and landscape, and is one of the most densely built American campus environments. . . .

3. Enhance the Central Campus

   The Central Campus, east of the Core Campus and bounded by Interstate 35, Martin Luther King Jr. Boulevard, and Dean Keaton Street, is significantly different in character from the Core. It is far less densely built, has less tree cover and more asphalt, and is less pedestrian-friendly. It offers significant opportunities for redevelopment and transformation into a natural extension of the Core. . . .

4. Forge Strategic Partnerships

Universities no longer thrive in isolation. Partnerships with adjacent stakeholders have the potential to advance UT's academic, research, and student life goals. Exploring potential city, state, and private sector partnerships for promoting and guiding development adjacent to the university campus and beyond is recommended as a priority initiative.

5. Facilitate Safer and More Efficient Mobility

Moving around the campus easily, comfortably, and safely is critical to the well-being of the campus community. Safe, efficient mobility helps ensure a vibrant academic setting, where connectivity and community transcend traditional disciplinary boundaries.

6. Transform the Waller Creek/San Jacinto Corridor

Waller Creek and San Jacinto Boulevard currently form parallel barriers between the Core Campus and the Central Campus. Rethinking how both the creek and the roadway can become enhancements to the campus rather than barriers is essential to successful improvement of the Central Campus. . . .

7. Improve the Learning and Research Environments

While the physical conditions for learning and research in individual buildings and the distribution of program uses around campus are not included in this first phase of planning at UT, the larger framework for creating an optimum environment for learning and research is considered, and essential background data have been developed. . . .

8. Integrate Academic and Residential Life

Student success rates are heavily influenced by residential and student life programs on campus. (Sasaki Associates 2012)

These ideas guided the preparation of the campus plan through the spring, summer, and fall of 2012. Particular attention was paid to floor area ratio (FAR) as a way to help realize some of the ideas.

## Floor Area Ratio (UT Austin)

As noted, the campus planning team concluded that the need for more and improved research and teaching will accelerate. To accommodate this growth, areas in the core, central, and east campus zones were identified for new construction and demolition (figure 24). The existing FAR in the core campus is already "one of the most densely built American campus environments," not that dissimilar from Columbia University in New York City. The magnificent collection of Cass Gilbert and Paul Cret buildings in the core UT Austin campus merit preservation. The aging buildings needed to be refurbished and repurposed. While some areas in the core were identified for modest FAR increase through new construction and demolition, the big change will be in the central campus. This part of campus will be transformed from a suburban-like setting to a more urban, walkable campus with greater FAR. Modest changes were envisioned for the east campus as well, but these would need to be negotiated with neighboring communities in a future phase.

## Town to City

My kind of plan helps guide growth to the most suitable locations while protecting environmentally sensitive and historically significant areas. Planners determine the appropriate fit of uses to locations.

I have been fortunate to apply suitability analyses to several plans. For instance, in the late 1970s I helped Whitman County, Washington, implement its comprehensive plan. The county's overarching goal was to protect its rich, productive farmland. The loess soils in the county are among the most productive in the nation for white wheat and lentils, and the Palouse landscape is quite beautiful. To preserve farmlands, essentially the whole county was zoned for agricultural use. The county leaders also wanted to provide for some rural housing. An analysis revealed specific opportunities for such housing that did not infringe on prime farmland and were not on environmentally sensitive lands. In the 1990s I worked on an analysis for Teller County and the City of Woodland Park in Colorado. Planners employed this analysis to help direct new developments to suitable places while preserving environmental and historical resources.

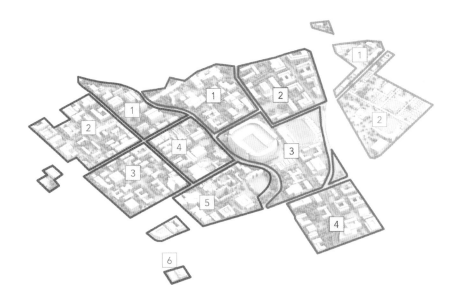

| SUB ZONE | EXISTING GSF | PROPOSED NEW CONSTRUCTION | PROPOSED DEMOLITION | NET NEW GSF | ZONE TOTAL GSF | EXISTING FAR | PROPOSED FAR |
|---|---|---|---|---|---|---|---|
| 1 | 2,048,323 | 502,683 | 219,523 | 283,160 | 2,331,483 | 1.9 | 2.1 |
| 2 | 3,905,350 | 415,636 | 211,675 | 203,961 | 4,109,311 | 2.3 | 2.4 |
| 3 | 2,809,119 | 55,092 | 4,951 | 50,141 | 2,859,260 | 1.6 | 1.6 |
| 4 | 1,892,756 | 204,501 | 110,995 | 93,506 | 1,986,262 | 1.4 | 1.4 |
| 5 | 3,514,786 | 154,000 | 0 | 154,000 | 3,668,786 | 2.0 | 2.1 |
| 6 | 459,819 | 0 | 0 | 0 | 459,820 | 6.0 | 6.0 |
| SUB TOTAL | | 1,331,912 | 547,144 | 784,768 | | | |

*FAR (Floor-to-Area Ratio) – a measure of building density, defined as the ratio of total building square footage to land area.

| ZONE | EXISTING GSF | PROPOSED NEW CONSTRUCTION | PROPOSED DEMOLITION | NET NEW GSF | ZONE TOTAL GSF | EXISTING FAR | PROPOSED FAR |
|---|---|---|---|---|---|---|---|
| 1 | 1,703,753 | 904,480 | 245,364 | 659,116 | 2,362,869 | 1.1 | 1.5 |
| 2 | 609,940 | 2,550,550 | 155,789 | 2,394,761 | 3,004,701 | 0.3 | 1.7 |
| 3 | 2,210,424 | 739,493 | 0 | 739,493 | 2,949,917 | 0.9 | 1.3 |
| 4 | 1,132,095 | 2,375,597 | 724,137 | 1,651,460 | 2,783,555 | 0.7 | 1.8 |
| SUB TOTAL | | 6,570,120 | 1,125,290 | 5,444,830 | | | |

| ZONE | EXISTING GSF | PROPOSED NEW CONSTRUCTION | PROPOSED DEMOLITION | NET NEW GSF | ZONE TOTAL GSF | EXISTING FAR | PROPOSED FAR |
|---|---|---|---|---|---|---|---|
| 1 | 238,587 | 0 | 0 | 0 | 238,587 | 0.4 | 0.4 |
| 2 | 274,611 | 378,002 | 0 | 378,003 | 652,614 | 0.2 | 0.4 |
| SUB TOTAL | | 378,002 | | 378,003 | | | |

Figure 24. Campus growth map and chart; image created by Sasaki Associates,
© University of Texas at Austin

The location of new development in the best places is fiscally conservative and fair. The protection of the environment ensures ecosystem services
for future generations: water is conserved and habitat for other species is
ensured. Likewise, the protection of historically important buildings and
landscapes sustain culture. In addition, historical preservation yields environmental and energy conservation benefits. Much energy is consumed
and greenhouse gas produced during construction. Rehabilitating existing
buildings can help conserve energy and reduce greenhouse gases. As urban areas expand, the balance of development and conservation is one of
the most important endeavors we humans undertake.

Austin has become a big city as Texas, the nation, and the world have
grown more urban. As has been widely reported, in the early twenty-first
century, the majority of the world's population lived in metropolitan regions for the first time in history. This urbanization will likely increase
globally, across the United States, and in Texas. In response, the city and
campus plans encourage density. The quality and character of that density
will largely be a result of urban, landscape, and building design. In my kind
of plan, design plays an important role in the realization of policy.

# 4 — DESIGNING OPTIONS

## AN EXPLORATION
## OF PREFERRED FUTURES

Design is not making Beauty / Beauty emerges
from selection / affinities / integration / love.
—Louis Kahn

According to Kevin Lynch and Gary Hack (1984, 127), "Design is the search for the forms that satisfy a program. It deals with particular solutions, while the program is concerned with general characteristics and desired outcomes. Design begins in the programming, and programs are modified as design progresses."

More broadly, the Carnegie Mellon social scientist Herbert Simon (1969, 55–56) observed, "Everyone designs who devises courses of action aimed at changing existing conditions into preferred ones. The intellectual activity that produces material artifacts is no different fundamentally from the one that prescribes remedies for a sick patient or the one that devises a new sales plan for a company or a welfare policy for the state. Design, so construed, is the core of all professional training: it is the principal mark that distinguishes the professions from the sciences."

Plans empower design. Often, this takes time. Every once in a while, plans prompt quicker action. Plans also stimulate design options. My colleague Danilo Palazzo of the University of Cincinnati School of Planning created the "Not Only One Solution," or NOOS, concept (see Palazzo and Steiner 2011). NOOS emphasizes that there are different possible solutions for each community planning, urban design, or development situation. Depending on the circumstance, many or few solutions may be possible. There may be an obvious best option or several good prospects. Planners should employ a flexible, adaptable process to define and select the most suitable solution, which requires adopting a structure and a strategy that enable the designer/planner to move toward a final target.

### Back to the Drawing Boards (Austin)

After the draft Imagine Austin plan was released to the public in the autumn of 2011, its advocates rallied support while its opponents attempted to torpedo its adoption. Because of concerns expressed by several neighborhood leaders and some citizens' advisory task force members, the city council's comprehensive planning and transportation committee decided the draft comprehensive plan needed more work. They directed the planning commission and citizens' advisory task force to undertake additional tasks and to make specific recommendations. The following seven tasks and recommendations were required:

1. review the action items developed during the working group process for the comprehensive plan elements and make recommendations to ensure those ideas have been adequately incorporated into the draft comprehensive plan;
2. identify potential inconsistencies between existing plans, including appendices of current adopted comprehensive plans, and the draft comprehensive plan;
3. provide community members an opportunity to request additional information and data for analysis of the draft comprehensive plan and help identify gaps in data analysis, if such gaps exist;
4. complete an analysis of the Preferred Growth Scenario Map based

on the sustainability indicators used to compare the Alternate Future Scenarios maps;

5. develop a method of tracking how the recommended action items relate to the policy recommendations within the draft comprehensive plan to provide additional insights on how the action items will advance the goals of the vision statement;

6. review and offer recommendations on amendments enhancing the performance measures and benchmarks within the draft comprehensive plan;

7. recommend a schedule for the completion of the comprehensive plan, including adequate time for review and discussion by the boards and commissions.

Much of the criticism directed at the draft plan concerned mapping. As I have noted, various maps could have been used more thoroughly and rigorously throughout the process. The revisions of the draft required by the city council prompted WRT and the planning staff to refine the maps. In several instances, the maps were amended to better reflect the suitability and compatibility of proposed uses with existing neighborhoods.

The planning commission and the citizens' advisory task force divided the seven directives and worked together to address the city council's mandate. Some five hundred groups and organizations commented on the draft plan. Each of the eighteen hundred specific comments and suggestions was considered by the planning commission and citizens' advisory task force, with help from the various responsible city departments. Considerable attention was paid to the growth concept map and supporting maps. From October 2011 to February 2012, fifteen task force and ten joint task force/planning commission meetings were held: twenty-five meetings over twenty-one weeks through Thanksgiving, Christmas, and New Year's.

As a result of these many meetings, leaders emerged from the ranks of the citizens' advisory task force, most notably Cookie Ruiz, the director of the Austin Ballet. She displayed extraordinary patience and resolve to move the process forward. Ms. Ruiz listened to all points of view and guided the participants toward consensus on often divisive issues such as development over the aquifer and balancing growth on the east and west sides of the city.

Jonathan Ogren continued to work on improving map quality. Ora Houston, Evan Taniguchi, and Mark Yznaga made significant contributions in thoughtful, measured ways through the many meetings, as did Frank Harren, a citizen, attorney, and real estate broker who attended practically every citizens' advisory task force meeting even though he was not a member. Dave Sullivan, Dave Anderson, Mandy Dealey, and Donna Tiemann especially kept the process moving forward with the planning commission. While these individuals provided leadership, others dug in their heels on single issues such as growth in the ETJ and concurrence with neighborhood plans. While some issues were indeed important, others were more trivial, like the wordsmithing of terms such as "mixed-use corridor."

Beyond refining the maps, WRT was not directly engaged in the task force and planning commission revision meetings. The city planning staff carried the load. As the draft plan was revised, WRT did contribute technical support from Philadelphia through weekly phone calls.

At its February 21 meeting, the citizens' advisory task force voted overwhelmingly to endorse the revised draft plan and send it on to the planning commission with a list of amendments and items for future action.[1] The planning commission held public hearings on March 13 and 27 and April 10, then voted 7-0 on April 11 to recommend the plan, with amendments, to the Austin City Council.

## Toward a City of Complete Communities (Austin)

The thrust of the Imagine Austin plan as it moved forward to the city council was to build a city of complete communities. The realization of that idea would rely on eight priority programs that each presented a clear design direction for the city:

1. Invest in a compact and connected Austin.
2. Sustainably manage our water resources.
3. Continue to grow Austin's economy by investing in our workforce, education systems, and entrepreneurs.
4. Protect environmentally sensitive areas and integrate nature into the city.

5. Grow and invest in Austin's creative economy.

6. Develop and maintain affordable housing throughout Austin.

7. Create a "Healthy Austin" program.

8. Change Austin's development regulations and processes to promote a compact and connected city.

As with the eight big ideas for the campus, these eight program areas would require major actions and decisions from the city council and city staff. Such operations frequently involve design. While parts of Austin are compact, much of it is spread out. Sidewalks, bike paths, and even roadways are fragmented and disconnected. Sidewalks end abruptly; bike paths begin in odd places. Surfaces are uneven and pavement broken. Austin's pedestrian and cycling systems beg for good design. A few good examples exist, such as Sinclair Black's Great Streets plan for downtown, which was being realized incrementally, with positive results (figure 25).

Figure 25. Second Street, a result of the Great Streets Plan; courtesy of Black + Vernooy Architecture & Urban Design

Water management had received considerable attention in Austin, with generally beneficial consequences. Still, Imagine Austin recognized that the region fluctuated between periods of little or much precipitation. With a growing, thirsty population, the city needed to design strategies to adapt to periods with scant rainfall while preparing for flash floods. For example, homes and businesses could be encouraged to use storm water collection facilities. Retention basins do exist throughout the city, but these could be more imaginatively designed, for the existing ones are concrete structures that attract graffiti.

Austin's economy is robust. However, inequalities exist. The growth centers concept was an Imagine Austin economic development tactic to help create employment opportunities for more people. Carefully designed centers would be accessible by transit and include a mix of live-work possibilities. During the planning process, an interesting and somewhat surprising concern emerged with economic and other consequences: food. Many of the young activists who attended public meetings and commented on the draft plan expressed strong opinions about food. They advocated farmers' markets, locally sourced food, and diverse eateries—all of which could be designed into the growth centers.

As with water management, Austin has a relatively strong record in other environmental issues. Imagine Austin envisioned that this would continue and expand. As city growth persists, environmentally sensitive areas will require protection, especially important aquifers and wildlife habitats as well as floodplains and productive soils. More ambitiously, the comprehensive plan suggested a better integration of nature into the fabric of urban areas. Such integration will prompt architects, landscape architects, and civil engineers to design in new ways. Brook Muller of the University of Oregon posits that such ecological design will be "one that creates more diverse urban habitat frameworks, filters and cleanses stormwater in order to improve biological conditions in compromised waterways, fortifies the connective ecological tissue of neighborhoods and regions, and in other ways supports broader, regenerative landscape processes" (Muller 2014, ix).

Austin is the self-proclaimed "live music capital of the world." A creative class is a challenge to generate and, even more so, to sustain, as migrations of young artists from lower Manhattan to Brooklyn and then on to Silver Lake/New Orleans/Detroit illustrate. Several artists and art institutions played a strong role in the new plan. As noted, Cookie Ruiz provided especially important leadership. Art interests are more prominent in Imagine Austin than in most comparable city comprehensive plans. Affordable housing is a particular concern to artists, who frequently have limited incomes.

Beyond artists, affordable housing is a broad issue in Austin. As more people have moved to the region, housing prices have increased. Poor and lower-income working people, musicians, and artists are especially at risk of being priced out of the real estate market. Part of the challenge is financing, and another part is design. Affordable housing can be integrated into new development through good design. The growth centers concept can help through a concentration and mix of land uses. In the Imagine Austin plan, the term "household affordability" is used and defined as the combined cost of housing, transportation, and utilities.

Health has been at the core of comprehensive planning since it emerged in the late nineteenth century and was codified and promoted through the 1928 *Standard City Planning Enabling Act* and corresponding Texas law. The new comprehensive plan sought to advance this tradition through the establishment of a "Healthy Austin" program.[2]

The other seven priority programs largely rested on the eighth: a new development code to create a compact and connected city. The existing code was confusing and outdated, but it was staunchly defended by some neighborhood activists because they could use it as a weapon to stall or prevent development. Certainly, some of this development should be stopped. However, the cumulative result is a sprawling and disconnected metropolis.

## Accommodating Growth (UT Austin)

As the campus plan was being developed, the likelihood of a new medical school became more promising. Senator Kirk Watson, UT System Chancellor Francisco Cigarroa, UT Austin President Bill Powers, and UT Provost Steve Leslie were especially strong medical school supporters. An Austin medical school had been discussed since the late nineteenth century. In 1891 the University of Texas Medical Branch was awarded to Galveston, then one of the larger cities in Texas, as a consolation prize for coming in second behind Austin in the statewide vote for the location of the university. After the horrible hurricane of 1900 destroyed most of Galveston, nearby Houston's population and economy grew more rapidly, and Houston became one of the most important medical centers in the nation. In 2008 Hurricane Ike, a Category 2 storm, caused extensive damage to Galveston and prompted discussion about downsizing the Medical Branch.[3] Meanwhile, Austin remained the largest city in the nation without a medical school.

In May 2012, at the urging of Senator Watson, the University of Texas System Board of Regents allocated $25 million in annual funding for an Austin medical school and another $40 million for faculty recruitment. Meanwhile, the Central Health District board placed a bond proposition on the November ballot to raise property tax revenue for Travis County residents in support of health care initiatives for Central Texas, including $35 million annually for a medical school.

On November 6, 2012, Travis County voters approved a property tax increase to support a new University of Texas medical school in Austin. Two days later, administrators from Central Health and Seton Healthcare, a corporate nonprofit and the largest health care provider in the region, met with the campus planning team. Central Health provides health services to low-income citizens. Seton Healthcare operates the University Medical Center Brackenridge, just south of the UT campus, and would share responsibility for the new teaching hospital with the medical school. The Central Health and Seton administrators were immediately impressed with preliminary schemes prepared by the campus planning team, including the idea to locate the new teaching hospital on UT property at the southern end of the central campus. On the spot, the health care administrators agreed to pool their University Medical Center Brackenridge property[4] and associated lands with the university to form a new medical district.

The first phase of the medical school district would consist of an administration building, the teaching hospital, an office building, a research building, a parking garage, and a chilling station to be built mostly on parking lots supporting a tennis facility and events at the 16,734-seat Frank Erwin Center, also called "the Drum." Both the Drum and the tennis facility were utilized by UT Austin Athletics and would eventually be displaced to accommodate the medical school district. The section of Waller Creek flowing through the district would be converted into a park-like corridor, which would complement plans by the City of Austin and the Waller Creek Conservancy[5] for the stream corridor to the south of campus through the east side of downtown. However, the floodplain would pose additional constraints for the UT Austin part of the corridor, which was viewed as a test case for a more naturalist landscape that would be adapted for other parts of the campus. In these areas, urban ecology allows for nature to come into the city a bit more through native plants and plant communities that replace traditional, manicured landscapes and invasive species.

The Frank Erwin Center opened in 1977 and has been a multi-bad-use facility: bad for basketball games, bad for graduation ceremonies, and bad for Lady Gaga concerts. The decision to build the Drum had generated quite a bit of environmental and community protest because of the neighborhood it displaced. The controversies are still recalled by many. The aging Drum would require considerable renovation, which would be as costly as building a new facility. As a result, the planning team suggested that it be replaced with a new arena in a different location to make way for the second stage of the medical district development.

## Revitalizing the Core (UT Austin)

Although the central campus would become denser, its character would also become more attractive, more like the core, including the historic forty acres, which is the most popular and memorable part of campus. Considerable attention was paid to enhancing the core campus and adapting its successful elements to new development. For instance, several courtyards exist in the core. The courtyards provide pleasant microclimates and gathering spots. Some are underused and can be improved. Other courtyards, such as Goldsmith Hall's Eden and Hal Box Courtyard, are popular and have spatial organizations that can be mimicked elsewhere across the university.

The Main Mall presented several challenges for maintaining and revitalizing the core. The Main Mall and the South Mall with its lawn are the focus of big university-wide events as well as many informal activities. We Americans love our grassy expanses. They dominate our most cherished places, appearing around our homes, in our parks, within our campuses, and across our golf courses. Lawn maintenance presents significant economic and environmental costs. Much of a weekend can be consumed attending to a front yard: mowing, trimming, fertilizing, weeding, watering, planting, and hauling away trimmings.

Beginning with the Lawn at the University of Virginia, most American university campuses have possessed significant symbolic open spaces, which come in many shapes and sizes. For instance, the South Lawn of the Main Mall is the University of Texas at Austin's most iconic open space. Paul Cret designed the mall to visually connect the university's tower with the dome of the State Capitol down the hill to the south. The Celebration Bermuda grass lawn is framed by live oaks and buildings. The South Lawn requires considerable maintenance, which is an increasing challenge with a shrinking budget and less available water as a result of droughts.

To make the South Lawn presentable for significant events like the spring graduation ceremony, considerable effort (and expense) is necessary. For instance, the turf used to be completely replaced annually at a cost of between $13,000 and $14,000. Meanwhile, many of the live oaks were planted around the same time. They will likely die together too. The South Lawn is sought after for various uses, and its intensive use has ecological consequences—soil compaction, for example, stresses the live oaks. Oak wilt disease poses another threat. Then there are the squirrels that also enjoy the trees; they chew on young trees and the fresh growth of older trees.

In planning the future of the UT campus landscape, there are at least four options for the South Lawn (if we rule out AstroTurf). First, we can accept the status quo. This option would acknowledge that the value of the mall for large-scale events such as graduation and as a backdrop for the Longhorn Network and other broadcasts justifies its costs. In addition, the mall possesses historical value that mostly merits preservation and, in the case of Confederate statues, debate and change.

A second option (and the one currently pursued by UT) is to adjust the management practices. UT has changed the ground cover below the live oaks, replacing the grass with hardwood mulch. The grounds maintenance team has employed a less aggressive lawn restoration procedure that may eliminate the annual turf replacement and does less harm to the tree roots. They no longer apply any synthetic fertilizers on the South Lawn (or anywhere else on campus). The use of organic fertilizers and soil additives such as compost and humates also improves appearance and drought tolerance. UT has also moved some large events away from the South Lawn while keeping it a pleasant place for students to mingle and for informal gatherings. This management approach should be expanded to include a replacement strategy for the trees, recognizing that they will eventually die. As the Sasaki Associates landscape architect Joe Hibbard observed, "The South Lawn should be viewed as a living landscape and not a tree museum."

A third option would be to keep the historical spatial structure but replace the Celebration Bermuda grass with a native species while also adopting a tree replacement strategy for the live oaks, which might include adding other tree species to enhance diversity. For example, Mark Simmons and other scientists at the Lady Bird Johnson Wildflower Center have developed a native grass mix called Habiturf. The blend includes three, sometimes four, native species: buffalo grass, blue grama, and curly mesquite, plus sometimes Texas grama. The advantage is that Habiturf requires far less water, fertilizer, and mowing and attracts fewer weeds than Bermuda grass. Although Habiturf needs less water and fertilizer, it does need some care. While less maintenance is necessary, a different approach is required. That approach would have some similarities to the steps UT Austin has already taken, such as the use of organic fertilizers. The Habiturf option would definitely conserve water. Tests done by the Wildflower Center show that Habiturf can stay green in the summer with only half an inch of water twice a month (2.54 centimeters per month). By comparison, according to the UT South Lawn irrigation report, the Bermuda grass there received an estimated 6.5 inches (16.5 centimeters) of water in August 2013. With Habiturf the water also can be stopped entirely, and grass will go dormant (but not die). It will then green up again once water restrictions are lifted or rain starts again. However, the biggest drawback to Habiturf is its lack of tolerance to heavy foot traffic.

Fourth, a radical departure from the current industrial lawn could be pursued. This approach could involve Habiturf but also mix in wildflowers. The rows of live oaks (*Quercus virginiana*) could be replaced by groups of oak mottes (*Quercus fusiformis*) like those that occur naturally in the region. An understory of plants could be introduced between the grass and the giant live oaks. Such a mix would result in even less water and fertilizer use and no doubt attract birds, butterflies, and other species. This approach requires a new, ecological aesthetic. A precedent is provided by the park of the George W. Bush Presidential Center on the Southern Methodist University (SMU) campus in Dallas. Designed by Michael Van Valkenburgh Associates with help from Simmons and his Lady Bird Johnson Wildflower Center team, the park employs Habiturf and other native species. The Bush Center's park provides a dramatic contrast to the manicured lawns of the rest of the SMU campus (figure 26).

For the South Lawn and other iconic open spaces at UT Austin and elsewhere, probably one of the first three approaches will be preferred. With increased concern about water, consideration of native grasses like Habiturf will likely grow. For new open spaces, the third and fourth approaches demand more consideration. Beyond design, UT's management of the South Lawn illustrates how shifting maintenance can improve the environmental health of a place. Successful landscape design considers factors like turf maintenance. All good design needs to balance several factors, including use, cost, aesthetics, ecology, and maintenance. The Texas drought that began in 2011 illustrated the need for a new ecologically based aesthetic. Native grass mixes such as Habiturf have much to contribute to such an aesthetic. The creation of a new ecological aesthetic for Texas landscapes presents a challenging and stimulating opportunity for architects and planners.

## The Search for Forms

One of the most important services a planner can provide is to help those who will be impacted by a plan to envision change and to comprehend its

Figure 26. George W. Bush Presidential Center Park; photograph courtesy of Lady Bird Johnson Wildflower Center

consequences. To be most effective in such presentations of the future, design acumen is essential. In the 1990s I worked with the City of Phoenix and several Arizona State University colleagues to plan the northern part of the city, called the Desert View Tri-Villages Area (Steiner 2008). As a result of our efforts, some 20,000 acres (8,094 hectares) were set aside in the new Sonoran Preserve. While this preserve represented a significant commitment to conservation, the balance of the area would be developed, some parts as urban centers, others remaining rural, and with some suburban areas as well. We speculated: could the suburban areas be designed better than the prevailing Phoenix metropolitan sprawl?

We noticed that some neighborhoods were designed better than others. We produced drawings that distilled some of the best practices: small front yards, large setbacks from natural drainage ways and rock outcrops, reduced street widths, low ranch-like buildings fitted below the tree canopy. These design principles and others were subsequently incorporated into the city's development codes.

My kind of plan employs design to help generate future options. Design is a creative act that requires an open mind. Design solutions are not premeditated, but emerge from an iterative process. Design thinking is based on empathy and partnership with those who will be affected by the outcome.

Design ideas are inspired by a variety of sources. For Paul Cret, his Beaux-Arts education provided the wellspring for his New Classicism. Our Sasaki colleagues drew on vast experience with campus planning at many other universities. For me, I recall the first time I picked up *Design with Nature*, which I saw during the first Earth Day on a table with a few other books by Barry Commoner, Paul Ehrlich, Ralph Nader, Rachel Carson, and Aldo Leopold. The environmental readings fit on a small table of the book fair, and McHarg's was the sole text with "design" in its title and a NASA photograph of the whole earth on its back cover. As a former Boy Scout who had been a summer camp counselor teaching art and nature, I immediately saw the appeal of McHarg's directive. Nature has inspired much great art. It holds the potential to stimulate new campus and urban designs. Decisions prompt designs; designs motivate decisions.

The decision is reached to make a parking lot a medical school, admittedly with scant review of any suitability other than proximity to the UT Austin campus and the existing hospital.[6] Meanwhile, a lot more new people need places to live and work across a metropolitan region. A new medical school on a parking lot or a new mixed-use complex in a growth center can assume a wide variety of forms. More than one solution exists. Current conditions, as Herbert Simon noted, need to be converted into a preferred future (or futures). Design explorations reveal possibilities for optional courses of action as well as visions for what can be built.

# 5 — SELECTING A COURSE

## A COMMITMENT TO ACT

The eyes of the future are looking back at us and they are praying for us to see beyond our own time.
— Terry Tempest Williams

Planning occurs in iterations, and by the time a course of action is decided on, the participants ideally are already pointed more or less in the same direction. As the future target is agreed upon, specific objectives emerge from broad goals. Such objectives can inform actionable steps necessary to realize the goals of the plan. As objectives are implemented, new conditions or ideas inevitably emerge and the process iterates, demonstrating elasticity. Gary Hack, the former PennDesign dean, observed, "Every planning effort is essentially a public learning process: discovering the possibilities, what will work in technical terms, and what can be supported by the beliefs, hopes, and fears of citizens and their elected officials" (Hack 2015, 222).

As Hack suggests, for a course of action to become realized, it must be adopted by some formal body. For a city or county, this is usually the responsibility of elected officials. For a university, various administrative bodies are responsible. In all cases in the United States, this occurs in a framework created by federal and state law. Cities and counties have the ability to protect the public health, safety, and welfare through the police powers granted to states by the US Constitution. These police powers are balanced with other rights, such as expression and property, as framed by numerous court decisions.

I like to always keep in mind my favorite amendment to the US Constitution: the ninth. It essentially states that no right included in the Constitution may be used "to deny or disparage others retained by the people." In other words, one person or entity cannot use their rights to property or free speech to depreciate those of other people. The amendment, of course, expresses the retention of any rights *not specifically enumerated* (as, e.g., property and speech rights are); that is, it establishes that one's right to free speech or property ownership may not trump some right claimed by the state but not specified in the Constitution.

Some objectives may be easier to achieve than others. Some may require that others be achieved first. Good plans often build on "low-hanging fruit" that can be picked relatively quickly and easily. Success helps breed success. The new medical district offered the prospect of a major victory for both the university and the city. For the university, the opportunity was to create a new kind of medical education for the twenty-first century. For Austin, the medical school would be the third anchor institution in the city's history after the establishment of the state capital and the university.

### Approval of Imagine Austin

As the draft plan moved ahead to the city council, planning members of the citizens' advisory task force and the planning commission remained engaged. Led primarily by Cookie Ruiz, we lined up support from many individuals and endorsements from twenty-six prominent local organizations, including the Downtown Austin Alliance, the local Congress for the New Urbanism chapter, Envision Central Texas, the Austin chapter of the

American Institute of Architects, Livable Cities, the Gram Parsons Foundation, and the Sustainable Food Center, to support Imagine Austin.

Meanwhile, plan skeptics ramped up their criticisms. Neighborhood activist Jeff Jack (who, as an ex officio member of the planning commission, had been deeply involved in the process, but had not gotten his way on every issue) called Imagine Austin "an elitist plan." Skeptics pressed three main issues. Neighborhood groups, led by the Austin Neighborhood Council (ANC), sought to eliminate or weaken language about implementing the plan through revising the city's development regulations. They feared such revision would undermine existing neighborhood plans. The staff, consultants, planning commission, and task force had worked to incorporate existing neighborhood and area plans into the draft, but ANC remained unconvinced. The plan's advocates believed such revision was necessary for implementation, one of the city council's initial overarching goals.

ANC also opposed the growth concept map (see figure 23, in chap. 3) and suggested that it be eliminated, which was the second remaining issue. The neighborhood groups were joined by some environmentalists rooted in the SOS movement of the 1990s, who opposed the few development centers in the western portions of the city over the aquifer. The map had been carefully drafted for equity to balance east- and west-side interests. The east-side groups, representing mostly minority populations, understood the water issue and recognized that the aquifer needed to be protected. However, it was not fair to locate all environmental protection on the west side and all development to the east. In addition, thoughtful regulation was envisioned for development over aquifer areas to protect water quality and for the creation of centers in East Austin that would provide needed jobs. The map reflected an attempt to balance these interests and thus was important for both fairness and implementation.

The environmentalists did support the fact that an extension to State Highway 45 (SH 45) was not on the map. The citizens' advisory task force had voted to remove it. This "Lazarus road" reappeared as a dotted line, added by the staff, during the joint task force/planning commission working sessions. The staff suggested that it would be a "green road." The SH 45 extension ran right across the heart of the recharge zone, and the only way

it would be green was if it was painted green. The joint group task force/
planning commission voted to take it off the growth concept map, and so
did the planning commission.

Still, the Chamber of Commerce and the Real Estate Research Council
advocated for the SH 45 extension, and it reappeared again as a dotted line.
In addition to the vague economic development reasons, the business interests argued that it was part of the past CAMPO planning, and that federal
highway funding could be jeopardized by eliminating it. However, funding
for the highway was far from secure. In addition to the environmental impacts, the road would contribute to sprawl and add to, not resolve, traffic
congestion. The extension would enable motorists and truckers on Interstate
35 to take Texas Loop 1, more commonly known as MoPac, through Austin.
One problem was that the MoPac bridge over Lady Bird Lake already served
a massive traffic catchment area and was congested much of the day. More
traffic would only exacerbate this problem.

With others (including former Circle C landowner and task force member
Ira Yates), I met with city council members and their staffs about these three
issues: rewriting the development code, the growth concept map, and the
extension of SH 45. Concerning the map, I recounted my experience with
Envision Central Texas a decade earlier. At the last minute, just before we
were to release the regional vision, ECT's board of directors voted not to
include a map.[1] This decision hampered the realization of the ECT regional
vision since there was no visualization of that vision. Eventually a map was
commissioned, which was largely adopted by CAMPO as part of its 2035
plan. I thought the Imagine Austin growth concept map was important to
communicate the plan and to advance its implementation.

The city council agreed. Their June 14, 2012, meeting stretched into the
early morning of June 15. After considerable testimony, the council voted
7-0 to make Imagine Austin the official city plan. The growth concept map
stayed, as did the policy to update the city's development regulations. Not
only did the SH 45 extension remain off the map, but councilperson Laura
Morrison successfully added an amendment to have the SH 45 extension
removed from the Austin Mobility Plan and the CAMPO 2035 plan. Overall, Imagine Austin defines the position of the city and reflects the majority
of community views on the highway.

"I want to thank everybody in Austin who contributed their time and creative ideas to Imagine Austin," said Lee Leffingwell, the city's mayor, after the vote. "Some folks spent two and a half years on the task force and countless others contributed their passion and ideas. This is a momentous achievement of working together to create a collective vision for Austin's future and we are committed to doing our part as a city to begin implementing this plan. We look forward to working with our partners and the public to make it happen."

Adoption of a new comprehensive plan launched an ongoing Imagine Austin planning and action program with an annual review of progress and a more thorough review every five years to determine if major updates to the plan are needed. "I'm excited about Imagine Austin," said Marc Ott, the city manager. "It is a flexible plan, so it will be updated on a regular basis. It will guide the values and decision-making for investments in the city and provide a context for the next thirty years."

## UT Board of Regents Approval (UT Austin)

Following a presentation by Larry Speck, the university's board of regents unanimously approved the campus master plan at their May 9, 2013, meeting. This came at a time when there was considerable tension between the regents and their flagship university. As a result, the unanimous endorsement marked a significant accomplishment. The approval also followed a $50 million donation from the Dell Family Foundation for the new medical school, which was named the Dell Medical School at the University of Texas at Austin. The campus master plan would contribute much to making the Dell Medical School a reality.

The campus plan included architectural design guidelines, written principally by Speck. The goal of these guidelines, he wrote, was "to provoke strong and innovative individual building design at UT Austin while at the same time creating a distinctive and pervasive sense of place for the campus as a whole. As most great university campuses demonstrate, compatibility and a holistic vision are not inconsistent with strength and particular identity of component parts."

The architectural design guidelines were based on "Ten Enduring Principles for Building on the UT Austin Campus":

1. Buildings should create well-defined public spaces.
2. The consistency of the fabric of buildings on campus should be tempered by exceptions that create local focus as well as campus-wide focus.
3. A wide variety of building typologies should be employed in response to varied programmatic needs.
4. Even as structures on the campus grow in size, they should maintain a human scale.
5. Buildings should accentuate and make visible the vitality and richness of campus life.
6. The broad palette of materials already employed on the campus should be used as a source book for future material choices.
7. Besides the colors that result from the use of natural materials, applied color can also be used as a means to animate campus buildings.
8. Building character should be responsive to the need to mitigate the strong sun and provide relieving shade in the hot Texas climate.
9. Durability, performance, and long-term sustainability should drive architectural character significantly.
10. Good value and practicality in terms of contemporary construction practices should be significant determinates of architectural character. The architectural character of new buildings on the campus should depict the university as a progressive and future-oriented institution.

Paul Cret had been a master of using buildings to create public spaces. He used the Cass Gilbert-designed Battle Hall and his own Main Building and adjacent Tower Building to punctuate the Main Mall and a series of three buildings with courtyards on both sides of the South Lawn (called "the Six Pack") to frame the most important public space on campus. The first enduring principle emphasized this space-making role of campus buildings.

The Cret and Pelli plans emphasized a consistent building fabric with spaces for more iconic buildings. For instance, Cret reinforced the consistency of the forty acres with the Tower Building, a campus landmark. The

Sasaki-Speck principles reemphasized consistency but made it clear that exceptions for local focus and campus-wide drama are possible and can make positive contributions.

The principles acknowledge the wide variety of building types that constitute a campus. Classrooms and wet labs have different needs and assume different forms, as do dormitories and parking garages, libraries and football stadiums, offices and power plants. For each building type, human scale is important to vitality and campus life.

The Sasaki team with Speck sought to draw on the rich palette of materials that exist on campus, such as limestone and a variety of bricks. By using these materials, future buildings would be visually connected to existing structures. Many positive qualities of the campus derive from natural colors. While the principles stressed the importance of maintaining this situation, they noted that "applied colors," an occasional purple, for instance, might be useful to accentuate spaces.

The principles noted that building design needed to respond to the Texas climate. Shade is especially important to mitigate the long spells of hot weather. Design for climate relates to building durability, performance, and sustainability, which in turn creates a long-term return on investment, as President Powers had directed the plan to consider. Finally, the architectural principles responded to an interpretation, a faulty reading in my view, that the Pelli plan mandated architecturally conservative guidelines. While the Pelli plan certainly paid homage to the Cret and Gilbert precedents, a broad interpretation was envisioned. In any case, the Sasaki-Speck principles plainly suggested openness to progressive architectural styles.

To ensure consistent and reliable conformity to the architectural design guidelines, the plan suggested the establishment of a campus master plan committee that has the strong professional and institutional knowledge required to evaluate compliance of proposed building designs for the campus. The committee would be appointed by the university president and would consist of the dean of the School of Architecture, two registered architects and one registered landscape architect chosen from the faculty of the School of Architecture, the chair of the faculty building advisory committee (or their designee from that committee), the director of the Office of Campus Planning and Facilities Management, and the vice president for university operations. All building projects proposed for the campus would then be presented to the committee at three different points: the earliest preschematic stage, the end of schematic design, and the end of design development.

Furthermore, the plan acknowledged that although it had laid the groundwork for the integration of elements such as academic planning, student life, infrastructure, and the campus landscape, more planning was necessary. The process of working through the first phase accentuated the importance of developing specific plans in a variety of areas not included during the initial stage. Several future plans and studies were envisioned (table 4).

Pat Clubb, one of the most persistent and persistently optimistic people I know, continued to be a strong advocate for academic plan coordination, as I believed a landscape master plan was necessary. Landscape design guidelines were needed to complement those for buildings. Everyone involved agreed that an East Campus plan engaging the neighborhoods across I-35 was important. As the new medical school would displace key sports facilities, an athletics master plan was needed. The goal to increase more on-campus student residences remained, but we had to determine how and where such housing could be realized. The university needed to continue to coordinate with the city on a variety of issues, including Waller Creek, the innovation district idea, and a variety of transportation issues. On the western edge of the campus, Guadalupe Street, commonly called "the Drag," presented an unsightly commercial strip. With increased residential development in the West University neighborhood, the Drag also posed safety challenges as large numbers of pedestrians, cyclists, and skateboarders with their ears plugged up by their music listening devices cross the busy street.

## Compact and Connected (Austin)

The first objective of Imagine Austin became to invest in a compact and connected city to create "a complete community." With a clear New Urbanism influence, this involved addressing transportation concerns, principally traffic congestion. The plan related traffic problems to the physical

TABLE 4. FUTURE PLANS AND STUDIES

**Academic Plan Coordination**

Coordinate individual academic plans, identifying overlaps and synergies.

Develop a template for integrating plans of individual colleges and schools.

Develop a comprehensive learning environment strategy, including assessment of
emerging learning trends and all learning space typologies, both indoors and outdoors.

Create an integrated strategy to support growth in research activity and interdisciplinary
collaboration.

**Landscape Master Plan**

Develop a comprehensive landscape master plan.

**East Campus Plan**

Include the East Campus in the next phase of master planning to engage the Blackland
and Upper Boggy Creek neighborhoods.

**Student and Residential Life Plan**

Develop a residential and student life plan.

Develop a strategy around engagement and investment in the West University
neighborhood as a major university housing village.

Develop a program-driven plan for the redevelopment of the Central Campus.

Ensure implementation of a plan for the revitalization of Guadalupe Street and invest in
providing student services in the West University neighborhood to make it a genuine
extension of the campus residential experience.

**Athletics Master Plan**

**City Coordination**

Coordinate transportation and mobility plans with outside agencies.

Explore the potential to develop a revitalization plan for Guadalupe Street and for
university investment.

Explore opportunities to create an innovation district in central Austin in collaboration
with the city and the state.

form of the city. Imagine Austin encouraged "complete communities." The growth concept map would be used to guide the city's capital improvement program, small area and transportation plans, and business incentive. Such activities would help make the city "less car-dependent and more walking, bicycling, and transit-friendly."

To foster a complete community, Imagine Austin identified seven building blocks: land use and transportation, housing and neighborhoods, economy, conservation and environment, city facilities and services, society,
and creativity. These building blocks were then associated with planning
elements (table 5). The building blocks created direct links to traditional
planning elements, as required in the city charter, but went further. New
elements were introduced for urban design; historic preservation; neighborhoods; children, families, and education; and creativity. Urban design and
historic preservation are rather standard planning elements. The neighborhoods element is a direct response to organized community organizations
through the Imagine Austin process. Children, families, and education plus
creativity present innovations in the Austin comprehensive plan.

## The Innovation District

Throughout the preparation of the campus master plan, UT staff and the
advisory committee met continually with various interest groups, including state and local elected officials and staff. These briefings were important to share information and reach agreement on key issues such as the
alignment of the proposed light-rail line through campus and the connection with the proposed Waller Creek park system. The proposed light rail
would connect major university cultural, athletic, and educational facilities to downtown Austin through the new medical district adjacent to
the State Capitol complex. The route also acknowledged that the center
of gravity of the campus had moved east from the Main Mall to Speedway
Mall and, with the new medical district, eastward toward San Jacinto and
Waller Creek.

An idea that generated considerable interest was the prospect of an innovation district. Sasaki suggested the concept, based on the success of
Kendall Square near MIT in Cambridge, Massachusetts (for an overview
of the innovation district concept, see Corneil and Gamble 2013). This
former industrial area has been transformed into a vibrant cluster of over
150 biotechnology and information technology firms. Innovation districts
mix uses near an anchor such as a hospital or research facility to foster
new ideas, new products, and new technologies (Mattson-Teig 2015). The

TABLE 5. IMAGINE AUSTIN BUILDING BLOCKS AND PLANNING ELEMENTS

| Building Block | Element |
| --- | --- |
| 1. Land use and transportation | Land use* |
| | Transportation* |
| | Urban design |
| | Historic preservation |
| 2. Housing and neighborhoods | Housing* |
| | Neighborhoods |
| 3. Economy | Economy* |
| 4. Conservation and environment | Conservation and environment |
| 5. City facilities and services | Wastewater, potable water, and drainage* |
| | Solid waste* |
| | Energy* |
| | Public safety* |
| | Public building* |
| | Recreation and open space* |
| 6. Society | Health and human services* |
| | Children, families, and education |
| 7. Creativity | Creativity |

*Source:* adapted from City of Austin 2012, 95.

*Required by city charter; in some cases, charter elements have been reorganized.

idea for Austin was to encourage start-up and biotechnology companies to locate near the confluence of a new medical school, a teaching hospital, the university, and the Waller Creek park system. The innovative district could take advantage of underused land adjacent to the new medical district in the State Capitol complex. With a rail corridor, transit-oriented development opportunities could be created at stops.

Much of the State Capitol complex is currently utilized for parking lots or garages. The state had struggled with what to do with its land and lacked a clear vision and sound plan. The Texas Facilities Commission, the responsible agency, had floated various options, including creating a public-private partnership around the Capitol in 2013. The thought was that the state and city would benefit greatly from higher and better uses, but the 2013 proposal was ill conceived as it involved selling off State Capitol land to developers for commercial development, including a forty-seven-story building across the street from UT's Blanton Museum of Art. Still, the new medical school and the Waller Creek parks provided an ideal opportunity for a well-planned innovation district.

My kind of plan depends on broad acceptance of the course of action by those affected. Our regular briefings about the campus plan with a wide variety of individuals yielded many results. For instance, in what we thought was a confidential briefing with the Austin mayor, the innovation district concept was introduced. He reacted with enthusiasm. Two days later, he featured the concept in his annual state-of-the-city address, which received broad media attention. Soon, business and civic leaders embraced the idea. Meanwhile, Senator Kirk Watson helped draw the rough area for the innovation district on the campus plan map so that it would be acceptable to state officials.

# 6 — TAKING ACTIONS

## A LIVE PERFORMANCE

Where flowers bloom so does hope.
— Lady Bird Johnson

Plans empower actions, or at least the good ones do. With a clear direction established, nimbleness is necessary to achieve goals and objectives. Actions require willful measures undertaken intentionally. Cities and universities have many checks and balances in place that help guide and constrain the conduct of responsible officials. Plans can grease the wheels of bureaucracies by stimulating new and renewed stimuli for action. Operations become the practical realities imagined through the planning.

Actions resulting from thoughtfully constructed plans tend not to be either arbitrary or capricious. Rather, measures based on clear goals, analysis, and participation—envisioned through design—are grounded in knowledge and empathy. Such acts are performed on a carefully constructed stage. In fact, we can use an analogy of a play or a symphony.

A script or score is written that becomes realized when it is performed. Likewise, a plan is composed and then fulfilled through actions. "All the world's a stage," after all, including a public hearing or a groundbreaking. Plans often unfold more like a free-form jazz performance than a carefully scripted symphony. As Shakespeare continued in *As You Like It* (act 2, scene 7), "And all the men and women merely players." The players—the planner, the designer, the engineer, the city attorney, the elected official, the university president, the citizen—improvise to the score or script laid out in the plan.

## The Medical District and Campus Landscape Plans (UT Austin)

Even before the first phase of the campus plan was officially adopted, planning for the new medical district began in the spring of 2013. That plan was approved at the same board of regents meeting as the overall campus plan (May 9, 2013). This set in motion the construction of the medical school with the goal to open it in the summer of 2016: a bold and ambitious act.

Following approval of the first phase of the campus plan and the medical district, work commenced immediately on a new landscape plan. The first realization of the landscape plan would be in the medical district. As a result, the landscape architect for the plan—Sasaki Associates, led by Joe Hibbard—would simultaneously undertake the landscape design for the medical district. Joe and Sasaki had prepared a campus plan for St. Edwards University (also in Austin), and he subsequently served as landscape architect for several building projects by various architects. This approach helped create unity for the campus landscape fabric, which was our objective for the new medical district.

A smaller leadership team from the campus master plan advisory committee worked with Sasaki and Larry Speck on the medical district. Pat Clubb, Steve Kraal, David Rea, Sam Wilson, Sharon Wood, and I constituted that team. Architects were selected and design began on the Dell Medical School education and administration building (opened in July 2016); a research building; a medical office building; a 1,120-space parking garage; and, separately, the Dell Seton Medical Center, which would serve as the teaching hospital (opened in 2017).[1]

Several key actions created the physical structure for the district. The curving Red River Street was straightened to make space for the hospital. In the process, the city grid established in the early nineteenth century by Edwin Waller was reestablished. Conceived as three distinct buildings in the campus plan, the research and office buildings were connected with each other and with the parking garage. This enabled the buildings to be located outside the Waller Creek floodplain. All the buildings would seek Leadership in Energy and Environmental Design (LEED) certification, and the district-wide landscape would achieve the new SITES status.[2] The development of the district involved a partnership between UT Austin, Seton, and Central Health. The vision for the district "is founded on an innovative idea for medical education that integrates healthcare, teaching, and research within an interdisciplinary setting, taking full advantage of adjacent university resources" (University of Texas at Austin 2013, 5).

An aggressive schedule was necessary to build the district from scratch and have it ready for students in July 2016. Seven principles were established in the plan that would help guide that schedule:

1. Nurture an emerging health and life sciences sector.
2. Forge strategic partnerships.
3. Create high-quality design and an attractive public realm.
4. Establish a resource for the Austin community.
5. Enhance connectivity and access.
6. Improve learning, research, and clinical opportunities.
7. Accommodate growth.

These principles were intended to distinguish the new medical school from other health science complexes. The medical school would be integrated, academically and physically, into the rest of the university. Although the number of students would initially be modest (fifty per class), room for future growth was necessary.

The medical district plan established frameworks for land use, the landscape structure, and mobility as well as three phases of development. The landscape structure provided an important urban design strategy that would differentiate it from other medical districts, which tend to have a large, impersonal scale and are often quite unattractive. The Austin district would have "strong landscape identity and cohesiveness," with "tree-lined walkways and streets that connect a range of shady court yards and plazas" that would "ensure an experience similar to the core campus."

As the team of architects designed the buildings and engineers designed the necessary infrastructure for the district, Sasaki both provided the specific landscape designs and prepared the broader campus landscape master plan and design guidelines. Completed in the spring of 2014, the overall plan laid out existing conditions, landscape structure and area guidelines, system guidelines, and policies. The plan identified seven landscape types across the campus:

1. Civic landscapes
2. Streets
3. Courts, quads, and plaza
4. Connective space
5. Parklands
6. Service and parking
7. Waller Creek

These seven types established a typology for thinking about and designing the outdoor areas of the campus. Grand civic spaces present different design constraints and opportunities than do service and parking areas, as streets differ from parklands. Waller Creek was called out for special treatment.

Concurrently with the medical district landscape plan, Sasaki revisited the 2007 Peter Walker plan for Speedway Mall—a potentially important civic space—and made suggestions to move that project forward. The project had first been conceived in the Pelli plan, which noted that the center of campus activity was migrating eastward. The Pelli plan suggested that the former city street become a mall and, as a result, the university closed Speedway at the East Mall crossing to all but emergency vehicular traffic in 1999. As a result, more student activities began to occur on Speedway, but the space was not ideal. The landscape architects Peter Walker and Partners were retained to produce a design, and they produced a transformative vision.

A major challenge of the Walker plan was its price tag: $120 million. Walker pointed out that many university buildings cost over $100 million.

However, this level of expense was viewed as excessive for what was super-ficially considered "beautification." Many of the costs in the plan related to unseen infrastructure below the former city street, which had become a cluttered remnant with scant resemblance to a campus of a "first class" university. The Walker design also addressed serious safety and parking issues. For instance, feral cyclists sped through the campus on Speedway, endangering students, faculty, staff, and visitors to places like the Blanton Museum of Art. In addition, the Walker plan included environmental en-hancements, such as reducing the area from 63 percent impervious cover to 38 percent and increasing the amount of green cover that would benefit water recharge and improve the microclimate. As large events were be-ing moved away from the South Lawn, Speedway became even more im-portant for student activities. With such uses likely to increase, Speedway needed to be redesigned to accommodate more student events.

The Walker design indeed would ultimately make the campus more beautiful by transforming an eyesore into a new green center, a move akin to the 1960s conversion of Locust Street, a vehicular city street, to much-loved Locust Walk, the primary pedestrian spine through the heart of the University of Pennsylvania's campus (see Puckett and Lloyd 2015). In my defense of the project, I noted to a local reporter, borrowing from Joni Mitchell, that we were "tearing up a parking lot and putting in a paradise."

As Thomas Jefferson illustrated in his visionary plan for the University of Virginia, attractive campuses enhance the learning process. The best and brightest students seek out beautiful places to learn. Many students decide the university they will attend moments after stepping foot on the campus. While the Great Recession that began in 2008 sidelined the Walk-er design in Austin, a generous gift from a philanthropist, Margaret Mc-Dermott, enabled the University of Texas at Dallas to hire Walker and his firm to redesign its campus. The results were transformative for UT Dallas, which grew in stature, becoming a cutting-edge educational institution, especially under the leadership of President David Daniel.

The Sasaki campus plan reinforced the Walker design and noted, "Of the many street and pedestrian walkways in the Core Campus, Speedway plays a particularly important role as a north-south pedestrian connec-tor. Redesigning the landscape and balancing the needs of pedestrians, cyclists, and service vehicles will improve the character of Speedway and ensure its success as a human-scaled and comfortable campus place."

UT Austin asked Sasaki Associates to study the Walker design in their landscape plan and consider ways to reduce its cost while maintaining its enhancing qualities. Sasaki suggested a strategy to rethink the infrastructure, specifically the drainage system. Walker had recommended a dual drainage system with a crown in the central path. Sasaki advocated a single drain. This and other ideas were presented to Walker and his team, and they agreed. He and his colleagues developed a new design that would cost approximately $70 million and could be realized in phases (figure 27). The new design adapted the Sasaki concept for drainage, with slight grades directing water to a center drain. We presented the revised conceptual design to President Powers on December 15, 2014. He remarked, "This will be what the University of Texas is supposed to look like, not like an extended parking lot."

"It'll provide an activity zone where memories are created," observed Pete Walker. He was given the green light by the president to refine the design. The board of regents approved the first phase of the revised plan at its May 2015 meeting and construction began in fall 2015.

Figure 27. Speedway Mall; image created by PWP Landscape Architecture

In the first phase alone, the number of trees increased from 150 to 290. The Speedway Mall project has become one of the most significant and transformative steps in moving forward two of the eight opportunities outlined in UT Austin's 2012 campus master plan. The opportunities, or "Big Ideas," include revitalizing the core campus and facilitating safer and more efficient mobility. When completed, the project will become an outdoor learning environment—a focal point of numerous campus activities and services which will enrich the experience of students, faculty, staff, and visitors under the majestic canopies of the mature oak trees that line Speedway. Table 6 shows the key features of the completed project.

TABLE 6. KEY FEATURES OF THE SPEEDWAY MALL TRANSFORMATION

**Pedestrian friendly**
Speedway will be a 36-foot- (11-meter-) wide pedestrian mall (includes two-foot-
   [0.6-meter-] wide flat curbs on either side)
No vehicle parking on Speedway
Vehicular traffic limited to emergency vehicles and vehicles necessary for conducting
   university business (restricted hours and locations)
No raised curbs

**Encourages alternative transportation**
Increased bicycle parking

**Encourages social interaction**
Plazas
Lounge areas
Space for food trucks

**Infrastructure supports university events**

**A landscape that is inviting and sustainable**
Improved conditions for existing mature oak trees
Additional trees
Native and adaptive planting
Increase in planted areas
Reduced impervious cover like asphalt and concrete

**Improved infrastructure**
Lighting improvements that enhance security
Improved storm drainage
Utility upgrades

### CodeNEXT and Light Rail (Austin)

A new development code named CodeNEXT and an improved transit system were two key implementation provisions of Imagine Austin. The city council organized an eleven-member advisory group in February 2013 to work with municipal departments on CodeNEXT, a form-based code approach. In contrast to traditional zoning, which is based on separating incompatible types of development and regulating use, form-based codes focus on physical form as the organizing principle (see Faga 2014). The following month, Opticos Design of Berkeley, California, was selected to lead a consultant team to work on the new code. Fregonese Associates, an important leader of Envision Central Texas, was part of that team. The code will determine "what can be built, where it can be built, and how much can (and cannot) be built."

By September 2014, the team had developed three approaches for reorganizing, revising, and updating the city code. The first approach, "The Brisk Sweep," provides a cleanup of the existing code "with targeted refinements and the addition of form-based standards that will have limited application, primarily to small area plans." The second approach, "The Deep Clean," "substantially improves the appearance, usability, and consistency" of the existing development code. The final approach, "The Complete Makeover," extensively modifies the existing code "by reworking its content and structure."

After these approaches were presented to the city council, the team began to draft the new code. Each approach contained a code format, development review models, and development standard models. Based on considerable public participation, the CodeNEXT team recommended "The Deep Clean" approach as the best way to implement the Imagine Austin plan.[3]

Meanwhile, the city advanced a light-rail proposal that was part of a larger transportation initiative. A bond was placed on the November 2014 ballot that would have built 9.5 miles (15.3 kilometers) of urban rail, including the segment adjacent to the new medical district and through the UT campus along San Jacinto. The measure also included $400 million for road improvements. The bond was opposed by antitax groups.

In some neighborhoods, voters could not see how they would benefit from the bond, a view reinforced by several city council candidates. The city had changed its council structure, which attracted a large pool of candidates. Several took an anti-rail position and drew their supporters to vote against the transportation bond issue in the city election. A few so-called pro-rail individuals were critical of the proposed route and were not shy about suggesting several alternatives, including a route on Speedway Mall through the campus, which was unrealistic because of infrastructure costs, the location of the Blanton Museum, the campus and Walker plans, and opposition from the university administration. These "pro-rail" individuals played a role akin to Ralph Nader voters in Florida in the 2000 presidential election. On November 4, Austinites defeated the urban rail transportation bond with 57 percent of the voters opposed. As a result, an important element of the Imagine Austin vision would go unrealized for the near future.

Still, the one rail line in the metropolitan region, the Red Line, which runs from downtown to the city of Leander for thirty-two miles (51.5 kilometers) with nine stops, continues to stimulate growth. The Red Line MetroRail stations illustrate the potential of the Imagine Austin centers concept. For instance, in March 2016 the Capital Metro board approved the development of the ten-acre (four-hectare) Plaza Saltillo station site in East Austin. This mixed-use development will include 110,000 square feet (10,219.3 square meters) of ground-floor retail space, 120,000 square feet (11,148.4 square meters) of office space, 800 apartments (at least 15 percent will be affordable), and 2.25 acres (0.9 hectares) of public and private open space.

## East Campus Plan (UT Austin)

The University of Texas has a checkered, mostly negative, history with its eastern neighbors in a historically African American community. For instance, one hundred black families lost their homes in the 1970s so that the university could build a new baseball stadium, a controversy that eventually resulted in an agreement between the university and the neighborhood group in 1988 establishing Leona Street as a dividing line between the campus and the neighborhood. In that accord, the university agreed not to expand east of Leona Street.

President Powers was committed to improving the relationship between the university and its neighbors. Recognizing that the planning for the area of the campus east of Interstate 35 would require considerable work with the adjacent community, detailed activity was taken out of the first phase of the overall campus master plan. Work on an East Campus plan began in June 2013, just a month after the board of regents adopted the overall plan. Sasaki cooperated closely with the Blackland neighborhood on the East Campus master plan, which was adopted by the board of regents on May 14, 2015. The neighbors as well as several university entities identified numerous issues related to athletics, parking and transportation, campus facilities, the university's child development center, the buildings housing UT Documents Solutions and the UT Press, student life, and neighborhood concerns. The East Campus plan was given urgency by the dislocation of the tennis facility to make way for the medical school. The Athletics Department desired to build a new tennis facility in East Campus. President Powers saw an opportunity to demonstrate his personal commitment to change the relationship with the Blackland neighborhood by creating a plan that addressed its concerns while meeting the needs of the university. The neighborhood concerns were described as follows:

- Leona Street should be improved as a welcoming edge, which could include graduate housing at a compatible scale, landscape enhancements, streetscape improvements, and neighborhood boundary identity features.
- Athletic facilities are supported only if they are not located along Leona Street; they must be set back and buffered by a compatible neighborhood use such as housing.
- East Campus development should step down in scale and height along Leona Street to be compatible with the mostly single-family neighborhood.
- Increased parking demands and vehicular traffic associated with new and existing development should be mitigated through the provision of a parking garage in the southwest area of the East Campus.
- The neighborhood could benefit from improvements to the East Campus that enhance its sense of place and identity.

- East Campus development should consider creating a neighborhood of graduate housing users along Leona Street who can be part of, rather than separate from, the Blackland neighborhood community.
- The Blackland Neighborhood Association submitted a resident permit parking application with the City of Austin.
- Expansion of the Facilities Complex beyond current boundaries is not supported next to the community edge.

Athletic facilities present a major neighborhood concern because of the deleterious effects of event parking. Fans regularly overwhelm on-street parking spots on game days. Neighbors were also worried about the scale of athletic venues and preferred residential and academic uses. Athletic facilities are often large, sometimes imposing on the surrounding area. Classrooms and student housing, the neighbors believed, could be more appropriately integrated with their homes and small businesses.

The Sasaki team worked with the university and the neighbors to agree on six principles to guide the plan:

1. Establish a planning and urban design framework that allows for long-term flexibility in the development of the East Campus.
2. Meet UT Austin's short- and long-term facility needs with uses that are appropriate for the East Campus location.
3. Enhance the quality of the built environment and create a sense of place through landscape and facility improvements.
4. Consider the concerns and community improvement goals of the Blackland neighborhood and East Austin.
5. Develop the East Campus in a manner that is consistent with the main campus master plan and the university's sustainability goals.
6. Ensure adequacy of parking on a campus-wide level as lots are displaced from the East Campus.

In addition to upgrading the existing softball and baseball stadiums, providing a new home for the Penick-Allison Tennis Center, relocating campus service units, and expanding the child development center, two big projects were included. Both undertakings reflected neighborhood desires. First, a new two-thousand-space parking garage was proposed. This garage will help alleviate parking problems in the adjacent neighborhood during sporting events and provide support for the day-to-day needs of the campus. In addition, the plan included specific game-day management strategies to mitigate parking impacts. Second, townhouse-style graduate housing was located along Leona Street, which included 538 micro units, 160 one-bedroom units, and 18 two-bedroom units. In total, these new buildings would house 734 graduate students.[4] The neighbors advocated such graduate housing, as it will complement the single-family character of their community. Considerable attention in the plan was paid to green space and streetscape improvements, which will benefit both the campus and the neighborhood.

Community leaders, who are often quite critical of UT, publicly praised the plan. Powers was singled out for his unwavering commitment to work with the community and address their hopes. "No other UT president has ever crossed the divide to understand the pain the people of this community have experienced at the hand of the university," said the longtime community activist, Blackland resident, and new Austin City Council member Ora Houston in an interview with the *Austin American-Statesman*. "You have to be intentional to lift up people. And [Powers] did that."

### Deferred Maintenance (UT Austin)

The Commission of 125 noted in the early twenty-first century that the "University has a backlog of critical maintenance and renovation projects, largely the result of the aging of the campus and inadequate resources" (Commission of 125 2004, 25).

The situation continued to deteriorate after 2004. The University of Texas has a large endowment, but it is spread across fifteen universities and health science centers. The system has considerable resources to build new buildings, but far fewer to maintain them. The situation was exacerbated by the tensions between the board of regents and the Austin campus. Many more significant issues, broadly described as "personal differences" between several regents and President Powers, drove the disagreements. Governor Rick Perry, who appointed the regents, believed that a university education could be provided for ten thousand dollars or less. Several regents agreed and proposed ideas, such as increasing online education, to reduce costs, even though there was scant evidence that such measures were effective or even less expensive. Gene Powell, the chair of the board of regents, praised Governor Perry's view, stating, "There was nothing wrong with getting a Chevrolet Bel Air–quality education as opposed to a Cadillac-quality one."[5]

The role of research at a research university was publicly questioned by several regents. In addition, a couple of the regents advocated significant increases in the number of undergraduate engineering and business students without new funding to offset what it would cost. Regent Powell supported raising enrollment at UT Austin by 10 percent every year for four years while cutting tuition in half. Whereas tuition was not reduced, the regents blocked tuition increases as campus building conditions declined. Meanwhile, state support for the university had shrunk between 2008 and 2015. Instead of raising funds for scholarships, deans increasingly spent their time finding ways to pay for fire-safety improvements, handicapped access, and air-conditioning repairs for buildings.[6]

The deferred maintenance did not go unnoticed. Letters to the *Austin American-Statesman* editor noted the fraying around the edges. Across the campus, doors and windows needed repair and/or paint. As a dean, I received missives from disgruntled alumni noting the eroded physical qualities of the School of Architecture buildings (such as water damage in the stairwells, peeling paint on the doorways, and missing and broken tiles on the courtyard fountain, which seldom works). Soon after one such message arrived, I happened to walk across the Stanford campus, observing an actual university of the first class and thinking about the gap between aspiration and reality in Texas, as reflected in the quality of the built environments at the two institutions. As Winston Churchill famously observed, "We shape our buildings; thereafter they shape us."

## Preliminary Accreditation (UT Austin)

However, big dreams can come true in Texas when there is the will. In June 2015, the Dell Medical School received its preliminary accreditation from the Liaison Committee on Medical Education. This established the green light for the university to admit its first class of students in 2016.[7]

"We are rethinking everything about medical education and the appropriate role of a physician in the community. As a result, we designed a school in which students will learn in ways that are fundamentally different from their counterparts at established medical schools—ways that, we think, represent the evolving needs and challenges of twenty-first-century health and health care," said Clay Johnston, the medical school's inaugural dean. "The accreditation shows that we have already begun to fundamentally change medical education in a way that is compelling to the medical education establishment."

Johnston had considered becoming an architect and possessed a strong affinity for design. He and Doug Dempster, the dean of the College of Fine Arts, established a Design Institute for Health. Johnston and Dempster recruited two prominent product designers, Stacey Chang and Beto Lopez, from the firm IDEO to lead the institute. In addition to being involved in planning a design of the new medical district, Dean Johnston enlisted our involvement in more detailed design.

Johnston felt that the empty-roof new research building was a lost opportunity. He sought our help for ideas for a green roof with research capacities. Mark Simmons and his colleagues at the Lady Bird Johnson Wildflower Center had conducted green-roof research that was specific to Austin's climate (Simmons 2015). Simmons, Danelle Briscoe, and I had extended some of those findings for a living-wall proposal for a campus parking garage (Briscoe 2014, 2015) (figure 28). That proposal had influenced a green wall on a parking garage in the medical district. Working with Sasaki, Simmons and Michelle Bright presented ideas for a green roof for the research building for research and demonstration.[8] These ideas were pursued and realized by the university's facilities, planning, and construction team. Dean Johnston had also advocated other green measures, such as including a cistern inside the parking garage and covering one of its walls with a curtain of vines as well as the restoration of the Waller Creek corridor. He especially supported pedestrian and cycling connections.

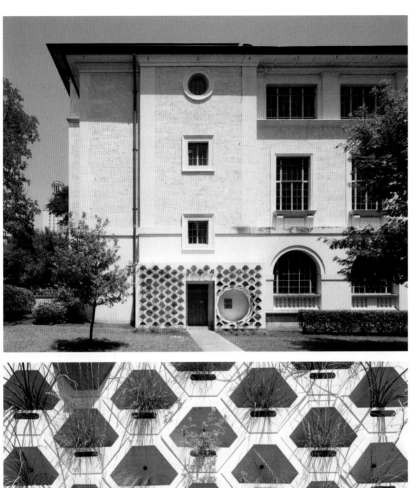

Figure 28. Living Wall: a. Goldsmith Hall; b. detail; photographs courtesy of School of Architecture, University of Texas at Austin

### Violet Crown Trail (Austin)

The Violet Crown Trail was conceived by several local activists in the late 1990s and advanced largely through the leadership of the Hill Country Conservancy, a land trust.[9] The trail utilized information from Envision Central Texas, the Trust for Public Land greenprint, and other sources and was consistent with the conservation and environment building block and element of Imagine Austin. The term "Violet Crown" used for Austin has been traced back to the nineteenth century (with much earlier references to Athens, Greece) in works by several authors, including O. Henry. William Cowper Brann wrote in 1891, "Austin's violet crown bathed in the radiance of the morning or arched with twilight's dome of fretted gold." Subsequently, Austin began to be referred to as the "City of the Violet Crown."

In 2010 the Hill Country Conservancy and several partners published a master plan for the trail, which was prepared by the firm Greenways, Inc. The thirty-mile (forty-eight-kilometer) trail was envisioned to begin in the heart of Austin in Zilker Park, extend through the existing Barton Creek Greenway, and then head south into Hays County. The trail will connect some 23,500 acres (9,510 hectares) of preserved land. The plan suggested that the trail would be realized in phases. The first six miles (9.7 kilometers) of the Violet Crown Trail opened in August 2015 and construction of the second seven miles (11.3 kilometers) began in 2016 and was scheduled to be mostly completed by the end of 2017. The trail and the associated protected lands represent significant green infrastructure for the city and an example of the potential to expand such amenities as envisioned and advocated in Imagine Austin.

The ideas about expanding green infrastructure were pursued in the fall of 2015 in the Hill Country Studio led by Potter Rose Visiting Professor Bob Yaro. Community and regional planning students laid out a visionary framework for the landscapes to the east and south of Austin. They recommended the creation of a Hill Country Endowment to promote education and research, conduct scientific analysis, and encourage design best practices (Hill Country Studio 2015). Yaro and his students observed that one of the best ways to protect the Hill Country was to build the Lone Star Rail between San Antonio and Georgetown (to the north of

Austin) in the I-35 corridor. By concentrating denser development along the transportation rail corridor and encouraging new development in the small towns of the Hill Country, its ecological, scenic, and cultural resources could be protected.[10]

"The future of the Hill Country and the Austin-San Antonio Corridor are inextricably linked," Yaro said. "Unless the water resources and natural systems of the Hill Country are protected, the economic potential and well-being of these big metro areas will be placed at risk."

Christy Muse is the former executive director of the Hill Country Alliance, an organization which works to protect the resources and heritage of that area. Muse noted the study addresses transportational, cultural, and ecological challenges that jeopardize the quality of both rural and metropolitan lifestyles in Texas.

"We have some of the most environmentally sensitive areas in the country west of I-35, and they are being threatened by suburban sprawl— growth from the larger cities that is increasing pressure on our water resources, our aquifers and springs, and could destroy the cultural lifestyle of our small-town communities," Muse said.

Other recommendations put forth by the Hill Country Studio included the following:

• Identify areas of growth and conservation through suitability mapping
• Identify desired urban utility boundaries
• Reform land development codes and policies
• Coordinate regional growth through a partnership of civic groups (Hill Country Studio 2015)

The studio team recommended near-term strategies such as generating scientific data, coordinating education and public outreach, identifying baseline indicators for tracking progress, and preparing model land development guidelines. Their planning framework also suggests creating a regional water authority and leveraging the resulting economic development to offset the cost of preservation efforts. If it were anywhere else in the United States or the world, the Texas Hill Country would probably already be a national park because of its natural and cultural beauty and environmental significance.

## Guadalupe Street

The university staff worked closely with city officials though the campus planning process. The campus plan envisioned ongoing coordination with the city, including the need to revitalize Guadalupe Street on the west border of the core campus. The Sasaki plan revealed that a third of the students, faculty, and staff walked or biked to the university. This relatively high percentage of walkers and cyclists (as well as skateboarders) resulted in large part because the city had upzoned the West Campus neighborhood.

As density increased in the neighborhood, the city adopted some unfortunate urban design standards, including retro lampposts that would be more appropriate for the nineteenth century (and even a questionable aesthetic choice then) and planters that functioned like plant coffins and sometimes created barriers for pedestrians. Meanwhile, safety problems for pedestrians and cyclists increased as the Drag grew ever uglier. The campus planning team suggested that the city pay more attention to Guadalupe Street and pointed to a well-conceived street renewal plan prepared by Sinclair Black in 2003. Unfortunately, the city took action with none of the urban design eloquence envisioned by Black.

In 2013 the city created a bright-green cycle track that separated bicycle from vehicular traffic. The segregation of bikes from parked and moving cars and trucks is a good idea. The green lanes added ugliness to an already unsightly corridor. The municipality also improved bus stops, another good idea, but in an attempt to create, in the words of the city engineers, a "landscaped buffer," more tree coffins were installed. Not all actions are positive.

Fortunately, two neighborhood groups reengaged Black in the Drag in 2015 as another study was being conducted by the Austin Transportation Department. That study was prompted by a city council resolution stemming from Imagine Austin. The priority elements for the Guadalupe Street Transportation Project include safety, transit, vehicles, environment, aesthetics/sense of place, parking, bicycles, pedestrians, and economic vitality.

## A Land of Drought Interrupted by Floods

Meetings morph into actions. As Imagine Austin and the campus plan were enacted, Texas continued to experience a significant drought, one that exceeded the drought of record from the 1950s. Fountains went dry and lawns turned brown. In response, the state adopted plans and the voters approved significant funding for water management that emphasized conservation. Then in the spring and again in the fall of 2015, significant rain resulted in considerable flooding that caused much damage and loss of life. Walls of water rushed through canyons, filling normally dry creek beds before engorging larger rivers. Central Texas historically experiences extreme weather. Those extremes are becoming even more drastic: the dries more parched, the wets more soaked, and the hots more scorching.

Imagine Austin and the campus plan initiated actions to adapt to and mitigate these extremes. For instance, the city and the university plans and designs for Waller Creek involve measures to improve water management and create oases of shade.

My kind of plan requires planting many seeds. Planners may sow kernels for the future through a variety of roles. In the case of Imagine Austin and the UT Austin campus planning, I was engaged in the whole process from before the efforts were officially launched through implementation. At other times my role has been more limited and strategic. For instance, in 2009–2010, the Canadian firm IBI Group retained me to help with the Mount Durmitor National Park Spatial Plan in Montenegro. Essentially, I was a technician (and to some extent was used to lend some additional academic credibility to the process). I helped with land suitability analysis from a distance and did not visit the spectacular mountainous park.

Some years later, in 2015, I traveled to Montenegro as a tourist. I still did not make it to Mount Durmitor, but I did visit two other of Montenegro's national parks (Skadar Lake and Lovcen). National parks are called "the green hearts of Montenegro." From local guides, I learned of the positive economic, cultural, and environmental benefits that derive from the five national parks in a relatively small country. The future of Montenegro rests with how its citizens manage their natural resources, which include stunning mountains and coastlines. Other nations face similar steward-ship responsibilities and opportunities.

The protection of the environment contributes many positive ecosys-tem services for people and other species. We depend on clean air and water and fertile soils. Conversely, environmental destruction creates negative consequences. As Pope Francis observed to the United Nations General Assembly on September 25, 2015, "Any harm done to the envi-ronment, therefore, is harm done to humanity. . . . In all religions, the environment is a fundamental good."

# 7 — ADJUSTING TO CHANGE

## A ROAD TO RESILIENCE

Change will not come if we wait for some other person
or some other time. We are the ones we've been waiting for.
We are the change we seek.
—Barack Obama

Plans propel ideas about shaping our futures in motion. Plans are produced by people who must realize the documented aspirations. Often, the more inspirational and elastic the plan, the more enthusiastically it is pursued. If the plan is for a neighborhood, planners may orchestrate a blueprint for its future, but its success ultimately depends on community inhabitants. If the plan is for a campus, it must be legible and relevant for new presidents, provosts, regents, faculty, alumni, donors, students, and staff.

Successful plans need to adjust to change. The direction should be clear, but the means to achieve the overall goals should be flexible and adaptable. Plans should have expiration dates when they need to be renewed or completely begun again. At UT Austin, the campus has evolved most pleasantly when new plans were formulated every ten to fifteen years. In

Austin, a significant gap in city planning existed between Austin Tomorrow in 1979 and Imagine Austin in 2012. While Austin prospered in many ways, congested streets, social inequalities, and suburban sprawl were exacerbated by a lack of a comprehensive vision.

A successful plan can generate an interest in more planning, even as it becomes outdated. Some cultures, such as those in the Netherlands and Portland, Oregon, are especially friendly to planning. Other places display less enthusiasm for public planning, such as Houston, Texas. Even Houston, though, has shining examples of planning successes ranging from the Johnson Space Center to the Buffalo Bayou and the Discovery Green. One can only speculate what as to Houston would be like if its leaders had embraced George Mitchell's ambitious green vision, displayed in the early stages of the Woodlands, the new community Mitchell planned and built with Ian McHarg and others starting in the early 1970s.

Uncertainty and change should not be viewed as barriers to plan, but as incentives. The future of our communities, the future of humanity, in fact, depends on our ability to adjust to change. Uncertainty is a fact of life, but science has helped us understand more of what was once unknown. Still we have much to learn. As Donald Rumsfeld noted, "As we know, there are known knowns; there are things we know we know. We also know there are known unknowns; that is to say, we know there are some things we do not know. But there are also unknown unknowns—the ones we don't know we don't know."[1]

Plans can be built on known knowns. They can acknowledge known unknowns. Hopefully, they can help prepare us for unknown unknowns.

## State Highway 45 Extension (Austin)

In spite of the city council's actions, the State Highway 45 extension would not go away. The extension remained a political football. Pro- and anti-SH 45 county commissioners were elected who either moved it forward or tried to stop it for good. Meanwhile, in 2013, Austin voters decided to change the at-large council to ten districts and an at-large mayor. The district idea had been advanced over the years as a way to increase diversity. However, by the time the new 10–1 city council district system was approved, the African American population had dispersed. As a result, black representation remained the same—just one person—after the 2014 election as in the previous system of six council members and the mayor elected at large. The number of women on the council increased to a 7 to 4 majority in the 10–1 system. The council did become more diverse in another way. Although officially nonpartisan, the at-large council had been dominated by Democrats. The 10–1 council included two Republicans and a Tea Partyer. The Republicans were especially sympathetic toward SH 45 (and were also anti-rail). One had included its extension in her platform.

If SH 45 was to provide an alternative route for I-35 through the city, then another north-south highway—MoPac—would need to be upgraded. As previously noted, the bridge over Lady Bird Lake presented capacity problems. Instead of addressing the SH 45/MoPac project as a single undertaking, the Texas Department of Transportation (TxDOT) divided it into segments (and thus avoided a comprehensive environmental impact statement). In February 2015 the Central Texas Regional Mobility Authority released plans for MoPac that included a four-lane expansion, a two-lane elevated platform over Lady Bird Lake and Zilker Park, and a flyover adjacent to Austin High School. The proposal was greeted with broad public criticism from neighborhood groups, environmentalists, elected officials, and others. As a result, the transportation engineers amended their designs. However, they remained committed to adding higher-capacity lanes, which many studies show only encourage automobile use, contribute to suburban sprawl, and discourage cycling and walking (see Frank et al. 2007; Larco 2116), and site-specific impacts remained negative.

In December 2015 the Texas Transportation Commission gave preliminary approval to the final $60 million loan necessary to complete a portion of SH 45 from MoPac toward I-35. The loan would be repaid from tolls on the road. As a result, the extension project moved forward in chunks.[2]

Among the project's drawbacks, the Lady Bird Johnson Wildflower Center would be adversely impacted by the MoPac extension. The major concerns were that the large increase in vehicular traffic on the high-speed highway would result in high levels of noise that would have substantial economic and environmental consequences. The center functions as a public botanical garden, wildlife haven, popular events location, outdoor recreation space, and native plant research and conservation organization. It is part of UT Austin and the School of Architecture. A 12-foot (3.7-meter) sound wall with a phony and ugly "Hill Country aesthetic" was proposed by TxDOT as a mitigation measure along the border of the center adjacent to MoPac. I wonder: in what parallel universe do these poured concrete walls represent the intrinsic beauty of the Hill Country, a landscape that is crafted and forged by bedrock, water, and people through time? These natural and cultural processes have established a craft, marked by local and regional distinctiveness, of building with local "found" materials and styles that are responsive to the environment. While I do acknowledge that we are living in a consumer-oriented society where mass production, efficiency, and cost and time (or lack thereof) drive decision making and that the fair city of Austin is growing at a staggering pace, I challenge the notion that we have to default, every time, to a one-size-fits-all mentality that establishes nothing more than monotony and placeless environment. What ever happened to site-specific solutions? What happened to design-ing context-specific solutions? What happened to our value of "keeping Austin Weird" (which I could interpret as meaning, "Keep Austin varied, diverse, context-specific, and appropriate to the here and now")?

I inquired about what mitigation measures would be employed to ame-liorate the negative consequences of the mitigation measure. With the generous pro bono help of Daniel Woodroffe and Eric Schultz of studio dgw., the spirit of Lady Bird Johnson was evoked in an alternative design with shorter, longer, more attractive, and more environmentally friendly walls and vegetated berms. The concept by Woodroffe and his colleagues involved visual and physical assessments and analysis of the specific land-form and vegetation conditions along the proposed section of Wildflower Center sound wall that resulted in ideas which actually celebrated and abstracted the sense of place, the character, and the ethos of this corner of Austin. Their solution proposed to meet (and perhaps exceed) the sound-abatement goals of the "cookie-cutter" wall by replacing the wall with a design that addressed habitat, ecology, and, most critically and uniquely, place-specific conditions. The alternative design involved using local materials, native plants, and existing landforms to ensure a more appropriate and better-looking barrier that still functions as an important piece of infrastructure. TxDOT rejected the approach and proceeded with its Hill Country aesthetically ugly sound walls.

## Plan Monitoring and Review (Austin)

Imagine Austin stressed regular evaluation as a critical feature for implementation. Ongoing monitoring by the city council, planning commission, city departments, and the public was envisioned. Two review mechanisms were put in place: an annual report and a five-year evaluation and appraisal report. The annual report includes the following elements:

- Projects and policies (including capital improvements) implemented and the alignment of those projects and policies with the goals of the plan
- An annotated matrix indicating the implementation status and benchmarks of each priority program
- The work program for the coming year
- Suggestions for updates to the comprehensive plan needed to respond to new issues and changing conditions, for consideration by City Council. (City of Austin 2012, 223)

The annual report is submitted by the planning commission to the mayor and city council at the end of each fiscal year. For instance, *Imagine Austin: The Way Forward 2013 Annual Report* provides key facts and highlights accomplishments in the year following the plan's adoption, from June 2012 to fall 2013. While not an exhaustive listing of every activity of all city departments, the report references and links to other city departments' websites and documents that can provide a greater level of detail. In 2013 the city government reported that it was moving forward on the comprehensive plan through a five-point program found in chapter 5 of *Imagine Austin*: education and engagement, internal alignment, regulations, public investment, and partnerships (City of Austin 2013, iv).

For the third point, regulations, planners reported that the city was active in its efforts to align land-use regulations with Imagine Austin. The following is a list of regulatory projects that were under way or completed that year:

- Land Development Code Update: As part of the City's FY 2012–2013 annual budget, City Council allocated funds to revise the Land Development Code in alignment with *Imagine Austin*, and Council unanimously selected a consultant team for this effort.
- Cases for Rezoning: Since *Imagine Austin's* adoption, City staff has begun to review requests for zoning changes for their consistency with the comprehensive plan.
- East Riverside Corridor Regulating Plan: On May 10, 2013, City Council adopted the East Riverside Corridor Regulating Plan to align land-use regulations with the East Riverside Corridor Master Plan's vision for a vibrant, attractive, affordable complete community in line with *Imagine Austin*.
- Airport Boulevard Form-Based Code Initiative: In 2012–13, City staff and consultants are currently drafting new land-use regulations (form-based code) for Airport Boulevard to support a vision for a more walkable, transit-friendly and vibrant Airport Boulevard corridor in line with *Imagine Austin*.
- South Austin Combined Neighborhood Plan: Beginning in 2012, stakeholders have attended monthly workshops to develop a neighborhood plan for South Austin. Using *Imagine Austin's* Growth Concept Map and policies as a guide, the neighborhood plan will provide a finer-grain vision and neighborhood-scale goals.
- Subdivision Standards and Transportation Criteria Manual Updates: To help ensure that new subdivisions support *Imagine Austin's* vision, the City is concurrently revising its Subdivision Regulations and Transportation Criteria Manual. (City of Austin 2013, vi)

The five-year report will provide a more in-depth analysis through "complete communities" indicators (table 7).

These indicators provide the framework for a comprehensive assessment with specific metrics to gauge progress. Essentially, the city decided to rate itself with specific performance criteria. This approach contrasts with the often-arbitrary rankings of outside groups. Down-to-earth factors would be assessed, such as residents who are overweight, impervious cover, live music venues, bicycle miles traveled, and new businesses started per capita. Performance and improvement can be assessed by city planners

## TABLE 7. COMPLETE COMMUNITIES INDICATORS

**Livable**

Households with children (tracked geographically)

Residential density (people per square mile)

Median housing values (dollars, by zip code)

Median rent (dollars, by zip code)

Cost-burdened households (housing, transportation, and utility costs)

Residents who are overweight/obese (percentage)

Community gardens/plots/local farms (count and acreage)

Citywide crime rates

Perception of safety (community survey)

Homeless count (annual point in time estimate)

Number of farmers' markets, farm stands, and mobile healthy food carts

Households one-half mile (0.805 kilometers) or less from full-service supermarkets/
grocery stores (percentage)

**Natural and sustainable**

Developed land (square miles)

Mixed-use development (percentage)

Impervious cover (percentage per capita and total)

Parks and open space (acres/acres per capita)

Water consumption (total water use and per capita residential)

Water quality

Air quality (nitrogen oxides and volatile organic compounds)

Greenhouse gas emissions (by sector)

Energy generation, percentage of renewables

Development within the Edwards Aquifer recharge and contributing zones
(square miles)

Development within the 100-year floodplain (square miles)

Households one-half mile (0.805 kilometers) or less from a park or accessible
open space (percentage)

**Creative**

Dedicated municipal funding for arts (dollars per capita)

Private funding for arts (dollars per capita)

Arts programs in schools and neighborhood recreation centers

Attendance at arts/cultural events

Money brought into economy from arts/cultural events

Live music venues

Households one-half mile (0.805 kilometers) or less from an arts/cultural venue
(percentage)

*continued on next page*

TABLE 7 *(continued)*

**Educated**

School attendance rates

High school graduation rate (percentage, by geography)

Residents with undergraduate and graduate degrees (percentage)

Standardized test scores

Enrollment in certification, continuing education, and lifelong learning programs

Households one-half mile (0.805 kilometers) or less from a library or community center

Households one-half mile (0.805 kilometers) or less from a school, public or private
(percentage)

**Mobile and interconnected**

Transit ridership (percentage of trips)

Vehicle miles traveled (total and per capita)

Average transit headways (minutes)

Bicycle miles traveled (total and per capita)

Sidewalks (linear miles and percentage of street frontages with sidewalks)

Bicycle lanes (linear miles)

Households one-quarter mile (0.402 kilometers) or less from an urban trail (percentage)

Households one-quarter and one-half mile (0.402 and 0.805 kilometers) or less from
transit and high-capacity transit (percentage)

Employees one-quarter and one-half mile (0.402 and 0.805 kilometers) or less from
transit and high-capacity transit

**Prosperous**

Employment density (jobs per square mile)

Economic output (dollars)

Job/housing balance (ratio of jobs to people)

Employment rate (percentage)

Tax revenue (dollars)

New businesses started per capita (dbas filed per capita)

Households one-half mile (0.805 kilometers) or less from retail and mixed-use centers
(percentage)

**A community that values and respects people**

Public safety response times (minutes)

Voting rates (tracked geographically)

Proportionality of arrest demographics (yes/no)

Households one-half mile (0.805 kilometers) or less from medical services (percentage)

*Source:* City of Austin 2012, 225–226.

and elected officials year to year and over a five-year period. These assessments will be available to the public.

This approach is innovative and presents many good prospects for the citizens of Austin. For example, the Natural and Sustainable Indicators reflect an emphasis on "green infrastructure," a concept that appears often in Imagine Austin. Green infrastructure has been advanced by the US Environmental Protection Agency and others as a strategy to enhance ecosystem services through multifunctional open-space systems. A leader of the WRT team, David Rouse, is the coauthor of an important green infrastructure book (Rouse and Bunster-Ossa, 2013). This concept is a potentially significant lasting legacy of the plan.

## Campus Master Planning Committee (UT-Austin)

The planning committee envisioned in the Sasaki campus master plan and approved by the board of regents was organized in the fall of 2013. In addition to the members suggested in the plan, a faculty member from the Cockrell School of Engineering, the director of sustainability, and a past chair of the faculty building advisory committee were included. The new committee evolved from the long-standing faculty building advisory committee, which had played an influential role since the hallowed days of Dr. William Battle, a longtime UT Austin faculty member and president, who was a leader in campus planning. That committee had functioned well at a time when the campus was smaller and most new buildings were funded by the state, the federal government (especially during the 1930s), and/or the UT system. But as expectations grew that deans would raise funds for new buildings, the overall process became more complex. These changes prompted two changes. First, Dr. Patricia Clubb changed how architects were selected. Each selection committee included the dean of the school or college, a faculty member from that school or college, a faculty member from the School of Architecture, campus architect David Rea, and four UT system staff architects and engineers. Pat Clubb and I served as ex officio members. This process had been employed to select architects for new engineering and business school buildings,[3] as well as for the medical district.

The new campus master plan committee was the second change. It assumed many of the responsibilities that had been undertaken by a subcommittee (chaired for several years by Larry Speck) of the faculty building advisory committee. The new committee was charged with ensuring the integrity of the campus plan. The committee addressed a variety of issues such as public art, cisterns, banners, and food trucks and details such as a bridge and handrails.

Essentially, many small, ad hoc incremental decisions were being made, with cumulative negative impacts. Hal Box, one of my predecessors as the dean of the School of Architecture, called this "institutional vandalism." Public art on campus was an exception. Through the university's Landmarks program, one percent of each new building project is set aside for art. The program's director, Andrée Bober, had put in place a strong process for selecting and locating art. She worked closely with Pat Clubb and David Rea to ensure that locations were consistent with campus planning and quickly wove that process into the functions of the new committee. For instance, the first piece approved by the new committee was British artist Nancy Rubins's *Monochrome for Austin* (figure 29), soon dubbed "the canoes" after it was installed in early 2015, because the fifty-foot-tall (15.24-meter) work was constructed of seventy aluminum canoes and small boats. The Rubins approval was followed by endorsements of thoughtful works by Marc Quinn and Ann Hamilton for the new medical school (figure 30).

But in other areas institutional vandalism flourished, always advanced by well-meaning people. With the drought, the idea of water capture from buildings spread across campus. However, cisterns often look awkward on a university campus. In Texas, cistern tanks serve a purely functional basis on farms and ranches but are ill suited to campus lawns, malls, and courtyards. The committee worked to find suitable locations for cisterns, including one in the new medical district parking garage.

Banners presented another challenge, as various entities on campus decided to brand their programs by hanging various drapes on their buildings or nearby light posts. The committee discouraged these random banners, but then student government leaders decided that the University of

a

b

Figure 29. Nancy Rubins, *Monochrome for Austin* (2015): a. detail; b. full image; photographs by Paul Bardagjy; courtesy of Landmarks, the public art program of the University of Texas at Austin

Figure 30. Ann Hamilton, *O N E E V E R Y O N E* — Zoë (2017); photograph courtesy of Landmarks, the public art program of the University of Texas at Austin

Texas did not have enough "school spirit" (which I had never experienced as a problem). Their solution was to circle the campus and line Speedway Mall with banners. Other students advocated food trucks and food carts.

More conventional items came to the campus planning committee. For instance, handrails were suggested on the steps of the Main Mall to discourage skateboarders and to improve access for disabled people. We also worked with TxDOT on plans to redo I-35 through campus and ongoing projects such as the new medical district and Speedway Mall. The Moody College of Communication proposed a new pedestrian bridge over a busy street to connect its buildings. The original bridge proposal looked like a gerbil tunnel. Instead, we helped select an architect for the bridge (Rosales + Partners) (figure 31), assisted with the necessary approval from the city to obtain the air rights over the street, and worked with Dyal and Partners on appropriate donor-recognition signage.

At the Zoning and Platting Commission meeting, the bridge was removed from the consent agenda because one commissioner thought it appeared to be an interesting project and wanted to learn more about it.

Figure 31. Moody College of Communication Bridge; photograph courtesy of Moody College of Communication, University of Texas at Austin

After five more hours, the pedestrian bridge design was approved unanimously with praise. At the city council meeting, one council person expressed concern about the potential for people trying to commit suicide by jumping off the new bridge. We provided the university's crisis management director, who presented data illustrating that there had never been a suicide attempt involving a UT Austin bridge and that there are no national data indicating this was an issue.[4] The council person was not convinced, but the bridge received approval. It opened in March 2016.

In addition, the committee reviewed and endorsed various other plans, such as the Division of Student Life's master plan, which proposed increasing undergraduate housing on campus, and the College of Liberal Arts plan, which envisioned an addition to one building and the remodeling of several others.[5] Both plans worked within the framework of the campus plan.

### A New Events Center (UT Austin)

University athletics were significantly impacted by the new medical district. As noted, the East Campus plan resulted in a new tennis facility. What to do with the Erwin Center remained an important question. From January to July 2015, the Athletics Department, led by Arthur Johnson, worked with Sasaki on a plan that included the location of a new events center. The facility would host concerts and graduations in addition to basketball games but would be slightly smaller (at least initially) than the Drum.

The process involved many on-campus and other constituents, such as the Longhorn Network, the band, and East Austin neighbors. Although off-campus locations had been suggested by both university and city leaders, only on-campus sites were considered. Several possible locations were explored and analyzed on the basis of various suitability factors, such as the State Capitol viewing corridor and walking distances for athletes and other students. An on-campus site to the south of the existing track field was selected. The facility would have 15,302 seats, with a possible expansion to 17,450. The campus planning committee endorsed the plan at our September 1, 2015, meeting.

## Waller Creek

Even though the Colorado River has been harnessed by dams, the creeks in Austin are subject to ravishing flash floods. The periodic flooding of Waller Creek hampered downtown development and reinforced the city's east-west divide. To address this issue, a flood control tunnel was built to capture and redirect floodwaters from the stream south of Twelfth Street. The $144 million, 1.5-mile (2.4-kilometer) tunnel removed 28 acres (11 hectares) of downtown land from the one-hundred-year floodplain and was completed in 2015.[6]

As ECT chair, I played a role in the project's funding. A tax increment financing (TIF) district had been proposed to pay for the tunnel. The TIF would use a twenty-year period of tax increases resulting from the undertaking to help pay for it. However, a TIF required support from both the Austin City Council and the Travis County Commissioners. For a variety of reasons, several county commissioners hesitated. The Downtown Austin Alliance reached out to me to help convince the reluctant commissioners. My ECT colleague Jim Walker and I were able to convince them that the TIF was a win-win opportunity; in fact, the county did not need to provide any up-front funding and would receive considerable tax benefits.

In 2011 several prominent civic leaders established the Waller Creek Conservancy to transform and sustain Waller Creek by "creating an extraordinary urban place that connects, surprises and inspires." UT Austin professor Allan Shearer influenced the conservancy and stimulated ideas about the prospects for the urban creek corridor. For several years, Dr. Shearer's UT landscape architecture studio focused on Waller Creek, with prominent conservancy board members—Melba Whatley, Tom Meredith, and Melanie Barnes—participating in the end-of-semester juries.

Shearer advocated a high-profile design competition, which the Waller Creek Conservancy board launched in November 2011. Competition guru Don Stastny was retained to organize and guide the process, which involved me as an adviser. A nationally prominent design jury was selected that included John Alschuler, Richard Haag, Carlos Jiménez, Marsha Maytum, and Darrel Morrison, with Shearer ex officio.

The competition attracted proposals from many of the world's leading landscape architecture and architecture firms, from the People's Republic of China to the Netherlands. Four finalists were selected in April 2012, each of whom received a $100,000 honorarium to create conceptual designs. After eleven months from the initial call for proposals, Michael Van Valkenburgh Associates and Thomas Phifer & Partners were selected and approved by Austin City Council on October 18, 2012, to design the master plan. In early November, Austin voters approved $13 million in the bond election for the Waller Creek development.

The Van Valkenburgh team concept involved a chain of parks with five distinct districts named the Lattice, Palm Park, the Refuge, Symphony Square, and Waterloo Park (figure 32). With the Austin bond approval and ongoing private fund-raising by the Waller Creek Conservancy, the Van Valkenburgh team began to refine their design from early 2013 on.

Following the board of regents' approval of the campus and medical district plans in May 2013, Sasaki began work on the landscape plan. Waller Creek provided a major focus of that plan in the medical district. Working with Bury Engineering, Sasaki translated its in-preparation landscape plan into a design for Waller Creek through the medical district. A goal of the medical district landscape design was to achieve SITES certification. To reach SITES standards and to create a pleasant and safe campus, several factors had to be considered. The first was the floodplain. Although the Waller Creek tunnel addressed flooding south of Twelfth Street, areas adjacent to the creek north of Fifteenth Street through campus remained subject to flooding. The masonry Fifteenth Street bridge with relatively small flow-through tunnels exacerbated the problem as it acts like a dam during flood events. The one-hundred-year floodplain helped determine building footprints for the new medical district and the location of pathways.

SITES emphasizes the use of native plants. The riparian areas along Waller Creek through the medical district contained considerable invasive, non-native species that would need to be removed. In addition, much native ground-level flora was missing because of shading. Some large-specimen trees—oaks, pecans, sycamores, and elms—were present, but were at risk because of bank erosion in their root zone. As a result, considerable restoration of the vegetative system was necessary.

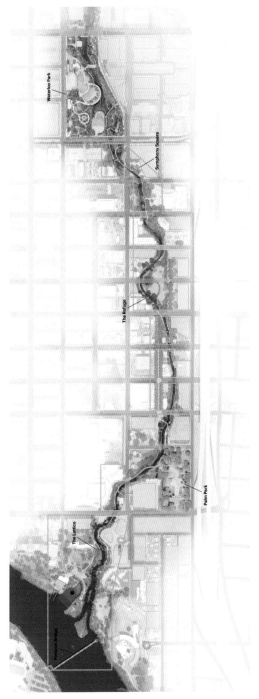

Figure 32. Waller Creek concept plan; image courtesy of Michael Van Valkenburgh Associates and Waller Creek Conservancy

The stream is also polluted. The storm sewer system of the campus conveys pollutants from paved surfaces and erosion sediment into the creek. Monitoring of the water quality in the creek reveals suspended solids, *E. coli* bacteria, and other pollutants, which affect biodiversity and threaten health.

In the campus landscape plan, Sasaki recommended the following steps:

• Transform the creek environment from a barrier to a linkage.
• Develop a continuous creek-side trail.
• Include educational signage about creek ecology and restoration along the trails.
• Use natural design practices.
• Remove existing structures.
• Remove rock-veneered banks that are failing.
• Fortify all existing structural bank/bed/channel solutions with bioengineered plantings.
• Create an upland savannah.
• Reduce mowing of lawns.
• Reduce the release of storm-sewered water directly into the creek.
• For all new buildings, parking, and paved areas, design with zero storm water discharge principles.
• Use best management practices to capture and manage overland flow.
• Install a dedicated "stream team."

Furthermore, to restore the stream channel's ecological functions, Sasaki suggested that riparian vegetation needed three tiers: groundcover, understory, and upper canopy; that fish populations should be improved; that significant and visible flora and fauna could be highlighted to enhance awareness; and that new habitat should be created. Such a restoration effort would require the architects, engineers, and contractors to adapt new construction techniques, compelling them to think in new ways.

These recommendations for Waller Creek were first employed in the medical district. Fourteen large trees needed to be relocated and transplanted. One live oak died in the process. Its timber, along with that from twenty-nine smaller trees removed from the medical district, was reused in the medical school. In the teaching hospital, local artist Mark Landers was responsible for transforming the live-oak timber into the new reception station. A slice of the tree also was transferred to the Jackson School of Geosciences, where its rings were studied for past climate fluctuations. Other adjustments were necessary as the district moved from planning through design into construction. For instance, the campus landscape plan advocated a continuous creek-side trail. However, the floodplain required that the trail alignments be adjusted for safety. We designed the bike and pedestrian circulation systems so they could be moved closer to the creek if a new Fifteenth Street bridge is built in the future.

My kind of plan calibrates with alterations that occur in its context. The campus plan adjusted to a new provost, new engineering and medical school deans, and eventually a new president who had been a member of the campus master plan advisory committee. Meanwhile, the city's governance structure changed, resulting in a new mayor and a new and larger city council. Only the city council member Kathie Tovo was reelected in 2014. She had played a leadership role with Imagine Austin and helped to shepherd the plan through the transition. Thus far, the campus and city comprehensive plan have adjusted reasonably well to change and setbacks such as the failure to move ahead on rail initiatives. Both plans continue to provide positive guidance for decision making.

# 8 — REFLECTIONS

## A CLEARING IN THE DISTANCE

Follow effective action with quiet reflection. From the quiet reflection will come even more effective action.
— Peter Drucker

In his insightful article "Reading through a Plan," Brent Ryan observes, "Plans continue to constitute the major printed currency of the planning profession, perhaps because the public continues to see plans as meaningful expressions of future intentions for a place" (Ryan 2011, 309). Furthermore, Ryan contends that "generating plans is perhaps the central creative act of the planning profession" (ibid.), and, drawing on Michael Neuman, that plan making is the act which "gave planning its name" (Neuman 1998, 216). The process leading to the creation of a plan can help us understand what Ryan calls their factual meaning, contextual meaning, and temporal meaning.

We understand—we learn—both by doing, that is, by making plans, and by reflecting (Schön 1983). Through experience, we develop a tool kit for future endeavors to help anticipate what kinds of facts are useful, to help read context, and to help value the time involved in the process. Experience should improve how we plan and design if we pause to reflect on what happened during the planning process. We learn through our successes and failures. We can also learn from the experiences of others and from past plans. Precedents, case studies, and war stories enable us to expand our understanding of what is possible. Travel can help us to learn and see the world from a fresh perspective as well. This can be especially true when visiting a place recovering from a natural disaster, such as a hurricane along the Gulf Coast, or from a recent war, such as in Croatia and Montenegro, where the wounds of the civil wars of the 1990s linger. In such cases, the resiliency of our species is evident.

As planning advances, should plans of today ameliorate the sins of past plans?

One of the more powerful aspects of Imagine Austin is the open acknowledgment of how past plans reinforced and even created racial divides in the city. Likewise, Bill Powers remained steadfast that the university's East Campus master plan would not only address mistakes of the past but also reflect the hopes of the university's neighbors for our collective future. Concerns about equity are intertwined with environmental quality. As the Kentucky poet Wendell Berry observed, "There is in fact no distinction between the fate of the land and the fate of people. When one is abused, the other suffers" (Berry 2012).

Plans should result in better environments for people to live in. In his architecture manifesto, *fit*, Robert Geddes provides a good summary of what people expect in our surroundings. According to the seasoned Princeton architect,

> We need an *understandable* environment . . .
> We need an *operational* environment . . .
> We need an *ethical* environment . . .
> We need an *aesthetic* environment. (Geddes 2013, 2–3)

At minimum, a good plan needs to meet the expectations of the community. More ambitiously, a great plan should serve the needs of future generations and other species. The jury is still out on the long-term success of the Imagine Austin and campus master plans. Time will tell. Still, there are indicators of success and of challenge.

Looking back over the plans discussed in this book, it occurs to me that plan making involves lots of list making. At some point, lists replaced maps as the principal tool for planning. Although these lists appear simple, even obvious, they are summaries of considerable discussion and thought. They represent consensus and mark a place in time.

Maps have lasting consequences, as the 1928 Austin city plan and the 1976 Lake Austin plan illustrate. The 1928 map resulted in a segregated and divided city that persists to the present. The McHarg maps helped create the leafy neighborhoods in southwest Austin and West Lake Hills. The influence of maps can be significant.

Lists have consequences, too. They can influence budgets that have far-reaching impacts or effects. Martin Luther King Jr. observed, "A nation that continues year after year to spend more money on military defense than on programs of social uplift is approaching spiritual doom."[1] King indicates that how a government spends its resources has ethical consequences, which makes a budget a moral document.

The consequences of the lists and policies in Imagine Austin and the University of Texas campus plan continue to be realized. The plans help frame and address new challenges and opportunities. Each year, progress on Imagine Austin is to be reported and assessed. The campus planning committee continues to review changes as they relate to the plans prepared by Sasaki and others. As has been noted, many endeavors overlap the city and the university and require cooperation: Waller Creek, the innovation district, the replacement of the Erwin Center, the East Austin and West Campus neighborhoods, and the challenges of transportation all serve as examples.

As progress continued on Waller Creek through the Dell medical district and in the city, the corridor needed renewed attention through the rest of the campus. For instance, the murder of a freshman dance major in April 2016 along the creek highlighted safety issues. Meanwhile, in September 2016 university officials discovered raw sewage from an engineering building flowing into the creek and resulting in chronically elevated levels of fecal bacteria. In the Sasaki plan, the future of the Waller Creek/

San Jacinto corridor rested largely on light rail. If the voters had approved the light-rail initiative, the line would have been built roughly simultaneously with the medical district. With planners and community groups beginning to coalesce around a possible Guadalupe light-rail route, the San Jacinto corridor needed to be rethought.

In addition, the Texas Exes began to reconsider their alumni center on San Jacinto. The Snøhetta firm was retained and prepared an ambitious and rather breathtaking vision for a new alumni center. Craig Dykers, a UT Austin alum, and his Snøhetta team's design engaged Waller Creek in a sympathetic and creative manner, as envisioned by the Sasaki plan. Meanwhile, the alumni center design underscored the need for a new post-rail plan for San Jacinto. Pat Clubb and David Rea initiated such a study in late 2015, which also addressed other campus roads in light of the Speedway improvements.

UT Austin, the Seton Healthcare Family, and Central Health formed a nonprofit organization, Capital City Innovation Inc., to attract startup companies and researchers. However, the innovation district rests largely on the cooperation of the Texas state government. Larry Speck led a team to rewrite the Texas Capitol Complex Master Plan. The Texas Facilities Commission planned for the complex to be transformed into an enjoyable public space. The central feature is the conversion of North Congress into the Texas Mall, connecting to the Speedway Mall on campus to the north. The mall will be a car-free, grassy, tree-lined event space. Such a civic space framed by state office buildings had been envisioned as early as the 1940s.

The 2015 legislature approved key elements of that plan: two new office buildings along Congress Avenue for state workers between the Capitol and the university; three blocks of the Texas Mall with associated street improvements; and nearly forty-five hundred new subterranean parking spaces and utility upgrades. These buildings and those which will follow will help concentrate state government functions along North Congress and, with the Texas Mall, provide stronger street-level connections between the Capitol and the university as Congress Avenue becomes Speedway Mall at Martin Luther King Jr. Boulevard. This concentration also frees up the vast parking lots and parking garages to the east near the new medical district and Waller Creek for the innovation district. The Capitol complex plan reinforces the compact and connected vision of Imagine Austin.

Interstate 35 continues to divide the city and clog traffic. To address both challenges, Sinclair Black proposed burying and capping the interstate through downtown and the campus. The capped areas could be used for parks similar to Rose Kennedy Greenway over the Big Dig in Boston and the Klyde Warren Park over the Woodall Rogers Freeway in Dallas (figures 33 and 34). Professor Black argued quite persuasively that adjacent areas would become highly desirable for new development and that the parks would help heal the city's east-west divide.

In the spring of 2015, Senator Kirk Watson announced an ambitious plan for Interstate 35 through the city that would include some, but not all, of Black's ideas. Our campus planning team worked with TxDOT and

Figure 33. Rose Kennedy Greenway, Boston; courtesy of Rose Fitzgerald Kennedy Greenway Conservancy

Figure 34. Klyde Warren Park, Dallas; photograph credited to Dillon Diers Photography/
OJB Landscape Architecture

city engineers on improving traffic patterns and enhancing the bridges over Fifteenth Street and Martin Luther King Jr. Boulevard. The Fifteenth Street Bridge over the busy interstate is especially important for the medical district. The MLK bridge will help make it safer for neighbors from East Austin, the university's students, faculty and staff, and visitors to cross the interstate on foot and by bike. The bridges provide an important opportunity to both improve safety for pedestrians and cyclists and enhance east-west conditions between the university and East Austin.

Frequently, concerns and criticisms are raised about the costs of projects labeled as "beautification." As Lady Bird Johnson observed, "Though the word 'beautification' makes the concept sound merely cosmetic, it involves much more: clean water, clean air, clean roadsides, safe waste disposal and preservation of valued old landmarks as well as great parks and wilderness areas. To me . . . beautification means our total concern for the physical and human quality we pass on to our children and the future."[2]

Meanwhile, ugly interventions often generate public ire. This was the case for a large tank that is part of a new chilling station necessary for the medical district. The chilling station was one of the first issues brought before the newly formed campus planning committee. David Rea presented the various options explored by those responsible for the chilling station and explained how the least-bad site was selected while costlier alternatives (such as burying the tank) were ruled out as financially unrealistic. Essentially, the tank was presented to the campus planning committee as a fait accompli.[3] Still, we suggested it could be masked with lots of plants and possibly used as a public art opportunity.

While it was under construction, the tank received considerable negative commentary in the press and on social media, including the following remarks:

> "I assume they're constructing a lighthouse."
>
> "Jeez, and I thought The Drum was ugly."
>
> "Fellow Longhorn friends who have attended our tailgate parties in the past: I'm sad to report an end to our era. Our tailgate spot from the past 15+ years is gone and the new UT Medical School cooling station has arisen in its place."
>
> "Somebody actually sat in a meeting room and said, 'You know what we should build right at MLK and Red River is an enormous tank with kind of strange panels on it.' Surely they're going to cover that up with something else."

Well, I had sat in that meeting room and, with others on the committee, realized that the tank would not be pretty. It was eventually covered with a metal skin painted light tan to somewhat reduce its negative appearance. The chilling station was necessary for the new medical district, which was being built at a rapid pace. The tank will provide a visual reminder that even utilitarian infrastructure projects have consequences for the character of campuses and cities. As Pope Francis observed, "We make every effort to adapt to our environment, but when it is disorderly, chaotic or saturated with noise and ugliness, such overstimulation makes it difficult to find ourselves integrated and happy" (2015, 147).

While the campus master plan committee had discussed the Confederate statues and other related symbols in the heart of the campus, we took no action. To undertake such action, careful analysis would be required that was determined to be beyond the plan's scope and budget. Other issues, such as a fair East Campus plan, were more pressing. This contrasts with Imagine Austin, which directly addressed the racism of past city plans.

However, a few of the plan's critics contend that instead of addressing the city's past racism, Imagine Austin perpetuates this heritage. For instance, the geographer Eliot Tretter of the University of Calgary asserts that the "plan reflected and codified the dominant New Urbanist vision that had been pursued in the city's planning efforts over the previous two decades" (Tretter 2016, 121). In doing so, Tretter argues, the plan was a tool of business and development elites (despite some opposition from these groups) and was implemented at the expense of some neighborhoods, especially minority communities (despite significant support and involvement from minority groups). From my perspective, Imagine Austin represents a sincere effort to create a framework for directing new development responsibly while addressing concerns of minority communities.

Back on campus, as noted previously, the successful 2015 student government leaders ran on a campaign to remove the Jefferson Davis statue. Xavier Rotnofsky, the student president, followed through with his platform promise and presented a resolution to remove the statue to the new university president, Greg Fenves.

Following the mass murder of nine people at the historic Emanuel African Methodist Episcopal Church in downtown Charleston, South Carolina, on June 17, 2015, by a gun-toting young racist, the UT statues became engulfed in the nationwide discussion about the inappropriate, discriminatory nature of Confederate symbols. The UT statues were vandalized, with graffiti scrawled in red paint that read "Black Lives Matter" and "Bump all the Chumps."

In response, President Fenves established the Task Force on Historical Representation of Statuary to review and provide recommendations on the legacies of the Confederacy on UT Austin's Main Mall. Greg Vincent, UT's vice president for diversity and community engagement, agreed to chair the task force.

The charge to the task force included the following directives:

1. Analyze the artistic, social, and political intent of the statuary on the Main Mall, with particular focus on the statue of Jefferson Davis, as well as the historical context that they represent.

2. Review the previous controversies over the Main Mall statues, particularly the statue of Jefferson Davis, with special attention to artistic and historical factors considering the university's role as an educational and research institution. In providing alternatives, a discussion of the pros and cons for each alternative from the perspective of students, faculty, alumni, and other important campus constituencies will be particularly useful.

3. Develop an array of alternatives for the Main Mall statues, particularly the statue of Jefferson Davis, with special attention to artistic and historical factors considering the university's role as an educational and research institution. In providing alternatives, a discussion of the pros and cons for each alternative from the perspective of students, faculty, alumni, and other important campus constituencies will be particularly useful.

"To that end, the task force should ensure its work accurately represents history, values the fundamental principle that all people deserve respect, and serves to ensure these principles are preserved for the benefit of future students," President Fenves wrote in his charge to the group.

I was a member of the task force. We presented our recommendations to President Fenves on August 10, 2015. Before that, we met weekly through July and early August and held two public forums that helped to inform those recommendations. The first forum occurred in the Student Activity Center auditorium on July 7. The forum organizers posted the following guidelines (box 2):

---

BOX 2. CONFEDERATE STATUES FORUM GUIDELINES

Each speaker will have two minutes to comment. You will be kindly told to stop once your time is up.

The forum is meant for sharing your opinions and suggestions. No questions should be asked until after all those signed up to speak have finished.

Please remember that while people have varying views about the statues, we should all be respectful of the person speaking and everyone else in the audience.

Finally, this is a venue for sharing opinions, not attacking individuals or groups.

---

About two hundred people attended and two dozen students, faculty, staff, and citizens spoke, while campus police monitored the activities and journalists scribbled notes and interviewed participants. Speakers packed considerable feeling and information into their two minutes. Two Descendants of Confederate Veterans supporters accused the task force of being a "steamroller of political correctness" and a "kangaroo court" because of its composition (presumably because of the number of African Americans who served on the task force).

Young African American students, alumni, and staff stated that the statues represented "harassment in the workplace." One declared that "black lives matter" and then asked, "Does my presence matter?" Ed Dorn, a former dean of the LBJ School of Public Affairs, noted that his family had lived in Texas since the 1820s and declared, "Jefferson Davis deserves a place in history but not a place of honor on campus."

One young staff member expressed concern about who would pay for the removal of the statues. Noting the university's thin budget, she hoped it would not come from scholarships or staff salaries. Dr. Vincent assured her that it would not. A young student offered, "Just let us know when to bring them down and I'll organize students and faculty to do it on the weekend, for free."

Emotions were intense on both sides of the issue. Those who spoke in favor of taking down Davis and the other Confederates far outnumbered those who wanted to keep them. Several African Americans expressed the pain they felt was caused by the statues.

Meanwhile, at Dr. Vincent's request, I presented nine draft options for the task force to consider:

1. Do nothing. When preparing an Environmental Impact Statement, a "no action alternative" is required because there are frequently consequences of doing nothing [which I thought was true in this case]. It is helpful to thoughtfully analyze the consequences of doing nothing.

2. Take down the bronze Jefferson Davis statue only, leave the pedestal blank, and keep the other bronze Confederate statues and the George Littlefield Fountain inscription as they are.

3. Take down the Davis statue only, replace it with someone more appropriate and relevant to the university's history and mission, and keep the other Confederate statues and the Littlefield inscription as they are.

4. Take down all the Confederate statues, leave all the pedestals bare, and remove the Littlefield inscription.

5. Take down all the Confederate statues, replace them all with more appropriate persons, and remove the Littlefield inscription

6. Same as either option 4 or 5 but ignore the Littlefield inscription.

7. Leave all the statues and the Littlefield inscription but add interpretation and/or art to create teachable moments about the horrible legacy of slavery.

8. Take down the Davis statue only, replace it or not. Leave the other Confederate statues and the Littlefield inscription but add interpretation and/or art to create teachable moments about the horrible legacy of slavery.

9. Same as either option 7 or 8 but ignore the Littlefield inscription.

Task force member Lorraine Pangle, a professor in the Department of Government, added two more:

10. [Create a] historical sculpture garden that would be ideally constructed as an outdoor extension of a campus museum, such as the Harry Ransom Center or the Blanton Museum, serving as a permanent exhibit on The University of Texas and the Old South. It would contain, on low pedestals, the Coppini statues of leading Confederate figures, copies of the inscriptions presently on their pedestals, a walking path, benches, and plaques that both place these works in historical context and raise questions for students and other visitors to reflect on. A wall with the Littlefield Fountain inscription might be made part of the sculpture garden as well.

11. Remove the worst piece, the statue of Davis, to a museum, preferably on campus. Near its present location we should place a plaque, noting its former presence there. We should then begin a considered process of moving other pieces and introducing new elements to better reflect the principles and aspirations of the university in the twenty-first century.

We combined Professor Pangle's item number 11 with my number 2. Another task force member, Brian Wilkey, the president of the Graduate Student Assembly, suggested another option: the removal of all six Little-field sculptures, that is, the four Confederates plus Woodrow Wilson and James Stephen Hogg. Professor Ted Gordon, also of the task force, added one more: reorient the main entry to the university to the East Mall (as had been suggested in the campus master plan) to establish a Diversity Mall on the East Mall. Gordon noted, "History is not innocent, it is the living foundation for the present." We then began to analyze the pros and cons of each option.

A second public forum occurred on July 15. Forty people spoke. The speakers were more evenly divided between community members from outside the university who felt the removal of any of the statues was an affront to their heritage and people within the university, mostly students and faculty, who were offended by the monuments to the Confederacy. For instance, one speaker compared removing the statues to the Taliban's destruction of historical artifacts. "Cultural genocide," he said, noting that his great-grandfather fought with Robert E. Lee. In contrast, a UT history student observed, "It is frankly ludicrous that black students have to walk every day past the statue of a man who considered them subhuman."

*Do the descendants of the men in bronze hold the same views?* I wondered. Some act like they do, based on their public proclamations at the forum and on social media. As a task force member, I received many messages, which ran the gauntlet from troubling through wacky and on to thought-ful. The Taliban were mentioned often. But Jefferson Davis is hardly Bud-dha, and no one advocated the destruction of the statues; rather, they simply wanted to move them to a less offensive place.

A rather consistent minority view for keeping the statues in place maintained that their presence helped teach the negative past. As the UT professors Al Martinich and Tom Palaima stated, "Remembering the long and inglorious success of racism in our institution and our society is . . . important" (Martinich and Palaima 2015). This view overlooks the pain the statues inflict on African Americans and downplays the fact that this "inglorious" history could be taught and acknowledged in more appropri-ate locations.

On August 10 we submitted our report, which analyzed the intent of the statuary, reviewed previous controversies, and focused on five options:

1. Leave the statues in place and add explanatory plaques.
2. Relocate the statue of Jefferson Davis and the inscription to the west of the Littlefield Fountain to the Briscoe Center for American History, the Blanton Museum, the Texas Memorial Museum, the Harry Ransom Center, the Littlefield home, or an exhibit elsewhere on campus.
3. Relocate the statues of Jefferson Davis, Robert E. Lee, Albert Sidney Johnston, and John Reagan and the inscription west of the Littlefield Fountain to the Briscoe Center for American History, the Blanton Museum, the Texas Memorial Museum, the Harry Ransom Center, the Littlefield home, or an exhibit elsewhere on campus.
4. Relocate the statues of Jefferson Davis, Robert E. Lee, Albert Sidney Johnston, and Woodrow Wilson and the inscription to the west of the Littlefield Fountain to the Briscoe Center for American History, the Blanton Museum, the Texas Memorial Museum, the Harry Ransom Center, the Littlefield home, or an exhibit elsewhere on campus.
5. Relocate all six statues and the inscription to the west of the Littlefield Fountain to the Briscoe Center for American History, the Blanton Museum, the Texas Memorial Museum, the Harry Ransom Center, the Littlefield home, or an exhibit elsewhere on campus.

The pros and cons of each option were described. For instance, the third option recommended removing the four Confederate statues plus the Littlefield Fountain inscription. The statues and inscription would be relocated at the Briscoe Center for American History or another suitable location on campus. This would "address concerns about honoring Confederate leaders, though it also places emphasis on the Wilson and Hogg statues that remain" (UT Austin 2015, 7). The report noted that more than thirty-one hundred individuals conveyed their opinions on the matter to the task force. Of those, 33 percent were in favor of relocating the statue of Davis, 27 percent were in favor of removing all statues from the mall, 33 percent were in favor of leaving them in their current locations, and approximately 7 percent suggested other options or provided other comments (UT Austin 2015, 3).

Three days later, on August 13, President Fenves announced his decision. Essentially, he followed the second option with some twists. The larger-than-life statue of Jefferson Davis was to be removed that weekend and relocated at the Briscoe Center, where its historical relevance would be explained. However, a temporary restraining order filed by the Sons of Confederate Veterans in state district court delayed the removal until August 30. On that hot Sunday morning a squad of television crews, print journalists, pro and con protestors, and curious spectators witnessed the event.[4] In order to maintain the symmetry of the Main Mall, Fenves determined that the Wilson statue, which stood parallel to Davis, should be removed as well and relocated elsewhere on campus.[5] As the task force reported, Woodrow Wilson himself had objected to being included in the Coppini statuary. The other Confederate statues and the Littlefield inscription would remain. The university would consider placing a plaque on the mall to provide historical context for the inscription and the remaining statues.

"As a public university, it is vital that we preserve and understand our history and help our students and the public learn from it in meaningful ways," Fenves noted. "Jefferson Davis had few ties to Texas but played a unique role in the history of the American South that is best explained and understood through an educational exhibit. The Briscoe Center has the expertise to do that."

The controversy illuminated the significance of public monuments in changing society. Stanford Levinson has observed, "What is written in stone has no necessary permanence unless successor generations can be successfully socialized to view granite as less evanescent than a flag wavering in ever-changing winds" (Levinson 1998, 139).

Subsequently, the president decided to move the offensive Littlefield Fountain inscription to the Briscoe Center as well. In line with best practices in historic preservation, the inscriptions on the Davis and Wilson pedestals would be shielded instead of sandblasted. "We're covering over history, rather than erasing it," President Fenves joked. The practice of placing a veil over the inscriptions both concealed and protected them and made them available for future study.

While Fenves did not suggest replacing either Davis or Wilson on their podiums, this did not prevent various parties from suggesting options. For instance, a petition was soon circulated to replace Davis with Mahatma Gandhi. In a thoughtful vein, Andreé Bober of the campus Landmarks program suggested retaining the Art Guys of Houston to randomly choose a person from campus to be memorialized in bronze, thus creating a monument to absolutely *everyone*.

## Prospects for the Clearings in the Distance

Imagine Austin was messy; Jeff Davis and his Rebel fellow travelers aside, the UT campus plan was much less so. The scales are quite different. Like with design, scale matters in planning. One has more control over graphic and product design such as the layout of a poster or a webpage or a fountain pen or an automobile than over a building or a bridge. Still, an architect exerts considerable authority on a building (less so when the building is bigger and more people are involved and the design becomes even more collaborative), as does an engineer with a bridge. Landscape design is even more complex, as the materials involve living organisms in addition to people. The best landscape designs envision "a clearing in the distance," as Witold Rybczynski observed about Frederick Law Olmsted Sr.

The same is true with planning as the scale shifts from a campus to a city or a region. I believe scale affected the performance of the consultants involved in the campus plan and Imagine Austin. Both WRT and Sasaki are highly competent firms founded by two icons of twentieth-century landscape architecture (Ian McHarg and Hideo Sasaki). Scale plus a difficult climate of broad public participation made WRT's task harder. Because of my affiliations with the Philadelphia school of design and planning, I had expected more from WRT, which was probably unfair. Imagine Austin lacked the strong ecological vision and innovation McHarg had contributed to Austin Tomorrow four decades earlier. However, in the long run, if Austin can advance the green infrastructure concept that David Rouse and his WRT colleagues incorporated into Imagine Austin, then the contribution will exceed competence and be quite significant.[6] Sasaki Associates' work exceeded my expectations throughout their involvement.[7] They consistently brought imagination and fresh ideas to the effort. However, they dealt with a much smaller (although representative) constituent group that was less contentious than the rowdy citizens involved in the city plan.

Larger-scale decisions can influence campus planning as well. Actions by the Texas state government especially have consequences for UT Austin. For instance, in 2015 the state legislature voted to require that licensed owners be permitted to carry their concealed handguns into buildings at public universities. The law became effective on August 1, 2016, the fiftieth anniversary of when an architectural engineering student climbed to the top of the UT Austin Tower with three rifles, two pistols, and a sawed-off shotgun and began shooting students, faculty, and staff. In addition to murdering his mother and wife, the gunman, an ex-Marine with firearms training, killed fourteen people and wounded another thirty-two. The carry law created the opportunity for more guns, with much greater firepower than that of a rifle or shotgun from 1966, on campus. To comply with the law, considerable debate and planning about where firearms would be permitted occurred. Students and faculty expressed their concerns about the safety and welfare consequences in various venues and media.

Such decisions beyond the local matter. Scale has consequence as well. I have had the privilege to practice my art at several scales. As there were many overlaps in time and space between the city and campus plans, I helped provide a bridge between the two efforts. I witnessed the considerable effort that was invested by many well-meaning individuals in both endeavors. I hope that the return on that investment will prove those efforts worthwhile.

Will Austin become more livable, natural and sustainable, mobile and interconnected, prosperous, creative, and educated? Will Austinites value and respect their fellow citizens? Will the University of Texas at Austin accommodate growth, revitalize the core campus, enhance the central campus, forge strategic partnerships, facilitate safer and more efficient mobility, transform the Waller Creek/San Jacinto Corridor, improve learning and research environments, and integrate academic and residential life? In the case of both the UT campus and Austin, time will determine the significance of my kind of planning.

# CODA

In preparing for battle I have always found that plans
are useless, but planning is indispensable.
— Dwight David Eisenhower

A plan is but one artifact of planning. Successful planning yields many
other results. Ideas from the planning process are realized in the built
environment through subsequent actions resulting in better places for
people to live, work, study, recreate, and worship. Lives are transformed.

As I moved from Austin back to Philadelphia, the campus and city plans
came with me (electronically), but, more important, the planning stays
with me (intellectually and spiritually). What lessons did I learn from the
Austin experiences?

- Do your homework, study the history of the place, previous plans, existing
  laws, and maps of everything. Places are layered with meaning. People
  have settled them with hopes which are sometimes realized, other times

not. They have left accounts of their settlement; recorded their plans and
expectations. Residents and scholars have studied the natural environment
and the cultures that proceeded them. A good planner will seek out everything possible that has been recorded about their planning area.

- Try to think in geologic time while imagining what may be clearings of
  hope in the distance. The planet predates us. Of the various geological
  eras, we are now in one of our own making, called the Anthropocene. As
  we navigate this epoch where our activities significantly impact the Earth's
  weather, geology, and ecosystems, it is essential to understand the deep
  structure of the places we plan. In doing so, we need to consider the consequences of our actions on future generations.
- Learn from past planning failures and successes. Every community has its
  share of both. A good planner will be able not only to identify what worked
  and what did not in past plans but also to ascertain what led to positive
  or negative outcomes. Often failures involve the lack of citizen support.
  Conversely, positive research results frequently flow from informed and
  opportunistic political leadership.
- Be bold and visionary but humble. "Make no little plans," the architect
  Daniel Burnham reportedly stated, continuing, "They have no magic to stir
  men's blood and probably themselves will not be realized. Make big plans;
  aim high in hope and work." Among others, Jane Jacobs (1961) and Robert
  Caro (1974) have illustrated the folly of (too) big plans not grounded in the
  desires of citizens. An ideal plan strikes a balance between high aspirations
  and firm grounding.
- Illustrate your plans generously with photographs, drawings, maps, and
  diagrams. People are visual creatures. Illustrations can help clarify complex
  ideas and proposals. Illustrations can also provide visualizations of what
  will be possible as a result of the process. Good planners possess graphic
  sophistication and/or appreciation.
- Write clearly and avoid planning jargon. (Your community probably
  doesn't need another "paradigm shift.") Planners and other professions are
  fond of their own terms, acronyms, and abbreviations. I recall from Latin
  that an alternative is one of two possibilities. Even though the definition
  has expanded over time to include more possibilities, for multiple prospects the word "options" often works better. "Stakeholder," when referring

to ordinary citizens, drives me crazy. Good planners write for a knowledgeable reader with clear prose.

- Listen, but be prepared to separate the wheat from the chaff. Citizen participation is wonderful, but some suggestions made at public meetings may be unrealistic. Some are downright nutty. A good planner knows how to spot the nuggets of gold in the theater of public forums. It's okay to have a point of view; planners are not expected to be potted plants.

- But know your role, play your role. As a professional planner, keep your politics to yourself. As a citizen, be political. Planning involves politics, but planners need to be apolitical in their official capacities. We must listen to and appreciate a broad range of opinions and remember that we are not elected officials. If we want to take a partisan political position, we should run for office. Service on a board or commission is a different matter because the appointment usually requires approval by an elected body. We should also vote.

- Roll with the punches; be adaptable and flexible but true to your values. Things will never go completely as you prefer. A good planner will be willing to compromise, especially on small matters (and knowing what is not all that important is an art in itself). However, you should remain loyal to your core values and be prepared to walk away from situations that are unethical.

- Keep a journal. The process of taking notes can help you remember who said what at meetings as well as the positions taken by various participants. A journal can be used to list ideas and possibilities. I often sketch in my journal, which helps me remember the mood of the meeting but also allows me to visually speculate about planning and design outcomes.

- Don't believe everything that is reported in the press about planning activities, but accept that it is (usually) a fair interpretation and that journalists try to get the facts correct. Planning meetings and hearings are often messy affairs with curious mixes of technical information and individual opinions. They can be emotional. Journalists attempt to make some order out of the chaos. Don't be surprised if you are misquoted, so be sure to choose your words carefully.

- Write press releases. (They can help journalists get the facts right.) Do not expect journalists to publish verbatim what you write (although they sometimes do). Rather, a press release can act as a fact sheet of source information for journalists and others. With social media, planners can post information directly. Good planners will be succinct and to the point in what they include. Illustrations and diagrams can be useful both for journalists and in the social media.

- Early successes help to realize a plan's goals. A plan can help nudge a project or policy already in motion toward a quicker completion. Such success can be credited to the effectiveness of the planning process. By the way, be sure to take credit for the successful project or policy.

- Early failures are not helpful. Sometimes a project or policy envisioned in a plan falls flat. A plan may even galvanize opposition. Some controversial and/or expensive actions either never happen or require considerable time and debate to realize. Also, own the failures.

- Keep planning. We wake up. Our minds begin to map out our day, our week, parts of the rest of our lives. We awake and begin to plan. That's who we humans are: planners. We need to apply this fundamental trait to how we shape our communities, which will in turn affect how future generations plan and live their lives.

# ACKNOWLEDGMENTS

Many individuals contributed to the campus and the city plans in Austin. For the campus plan, Pat Clubb provided the overall leadership with considerable patience and determination and David Rea ensured that things got done effectively. Larry Speck played a vital role from helping to initiate the plan through the realization of its implementation. In the midst of the Great Recession, Bill Powers made the bold decision that the plan was necessary. Bill's support of my involvement and Pat, David, and Larry's collaborations are much appreciated.

From Sasaki in Watertown, Massachusetts, key participants included Dan Kenney, Philip Parsons, Philip Perlin, Janne Corneil, and Joe Hibbard. Pat Clubb and I cochaired the planning advisory committee. The other members included Dean Almy, Tom Dison, Greg Fenves, Tom Gilligan, Ted Gordon, Bob Harkins, Julie Hooper, Brent Iverson, Sean Kennaugh, Steve Kraal, Philip Ladeau, Chris Plonsky, David Rea, Dan Slesnick, Jim Walker, Simone Wicha, Sam Wilson, and Sharon Wood.

After the board of regents approved the plan, a campus master plan committee was formed, which I chair. The other members were Kevin Alter, Pat Clubb, Elizabeth Danze, Robert Gilbert, Brian E. Roberts, Allan Shearer, Daniel Slesnick, and Jim Walker. At UT System, Jim Shackelford and Bob Rawski have played steady, positive roles in campus planning.

I served on the Task Force on Historical Representation of Statuary at UT Austin with Greg Vincent (chair), Laura Beckworth, Daina Berry, Hector de Leon, Ted Gordon, Rohit Mandalapu, Carlos Martinez, Lorraine Pangle, Xavier Rotnofsky, Marisa Swanson, and Brian Wilkey.

The Imagine Austin process was coordinated by Garner Stoll, Matt Dugan, and Greg Claxton from the city planning staff. The leaders of the citizens' task force were Margaret Cooper (formally) and Cookie Ruiz (informally). The other members were Greg Bourgeois, Roger Cauvin, Perlas Cavazos, Scooter Cheatham, Kent Collins, Patricia Dabbert, Rob D'Amico, Wilhelmina Delco, Greg M. Esparza, Frances Ferguson, Cecilia "Ceci" Gratias, Lawrence Gross Jr., Jack Gullahorn, Roland Hayes, Mari Hernandez, William Hilgers, Ora Houston, John Langmore, Mark Lind, Roberto Martinez, Frances McIntyre, Jennifer McPhail, Rebecca Melancon, Charles Miles, Karl-Thomas Musselman, Jonathan Ogren, Juan Padilla, Lori Cervenak Renteria, Jose "Danny" Rodriguez, Regina Rogoff, Evan Taniguchi, Donna Tiemann, Candice Wade, Allen Weeks, Jerry Winetroub, Ira Yates, and Mark Yznaga.

Dave Sullivan, the Austin planning commission chair, played a pivotal, constructive role, as did members Dave Anderson, Mandy Dealey, and Donna Tiemann. The other members of the planning commission were Richard Hatfield, Alfonso Hernandez, Saundra Kirk, Jean Stevens, and, ex officio, Jeff Jack.

From WRT in Philadelphia, the principal planners were Dave Rouse and John Fernsler. Their local consultant, Amelia Sondgeroth, made important contributions too. The city council at the time Imagine Austin was adopted consisted of Austin's mayor, Lee Leffingwell; the mayor pro tem, Sheryl Cole; and Chris Riley, Mike Martinez, Kathie Tovo, Laura Morrison, and William Spelman. Riley paid special attention to the urban design implications of the plan, while Tovo and Morrison ensured that neighborhood interests were protected. Cole was the strongest advocate for Waller Creek. Marc Ott, the city manager, and Sue Edwards, the assistant city manager, contributed crucial leadership.

Barbara Faga, Barbara Hoidn, Jonathan Ogren, Danilo Palazzo, Sandi Rosenbloom, Garner Stoll, Jim Walker, Barbara Brown Wilson, Jane

Winslow, and Daniel Woodroffe made constructive suggestions and helpful fact checks on drafts of this book. The two University of Texas Press readers also provided focused, constructive advice.

I enjoyed working again with the University of Texas Press, in particular Robert Devens, Sarah Rosen McGavick and Nancy Bryan. John Brenner did a superb job with the copyediting.

At the University of Texas at Austin School of Architecture, Chris Marcin provided ongoing support and assistance. Shannon Harris and Judy Parker typed several drafts, for which I am grateful. At PennDesign, Kait Ellis, Michael Grant, and Abraham Roisman helped bring this project across the finish line.

ACKNOWLEDGMENTS

# NOTES

## INTRODUCTION

1. This is a paraphrase of a remark often misattributed to Charles Darwin. I first saw it on a T-shirt at the Charles Darwin Research Station gift shop in the Galápagos Islands. Even though Charles Darwin never proclaimed this, the idea still rings true.

## CHAPTER 1 — SETTING GOALS

1. "Playboy Interview: Steve Jobs," *Playboy* (February 1985).
2. For instance, in the QS world ranking of architecture schools, Stanford was ranked thirtieth. However, Stanford does not have an architecture school, nor does it offer a professional degree in architecture. Stanford has an architectural design major in its School of Engineering. Princeton's nonexistent law school similarly fares well in rankings.
3. The grid was not true north-south, as it followed the ridge line. The grid is slightly southwest to northeast.
4. Austin was not the only southern city to enact such racial separation through planning. For Atlanta's history, see Lands 2009.
5. Fortunately, several blocks of Great Streets now have been realized, with many more to go, and the commuter rail line did open in March 2010. In fact, while Great Streets was tardy in terms of implementation, it is now a huge success story. Great Streets has transformed significant parts of downtown Austin, with many more blocks in the city in urgent need of a facelift or, better yet, a heart transplant.
6. Rouse left WRT to become managing director of research for the American Planning Association. He earned a master's degree in landscape architecture from the University of Massachusetts and a bachelor's degree in history and botany from Harvard. Fernsler earned master's degrees in city planning and architecture at the University of

Pennsylvania and a Bachelor of Architecture degree from Tulane University. Stoll had been the planning director for several cities before he joined the Austin staff and had received a master's degree in city and regional planning from the University of Oklahoma. Dugan had his planning degree from Virginia Commonwealth University, with a bachelor's degree in economics from UT Austin. Now with the Metro Nashville Planning Commission, Claxton had received his master's degree in planning from the University of Michigan and his undergraduate degree in sociology from the University of Maryland.

7. The US Census Bureau estimated Austin's population as of 2016 at 931,830. So far, the Austin planning area has grown a bit faster than the numbers used during the planning process.

8. A stream flowing from the north of the campus through its eastern portion, then south along the edge of the State Capitol office complex and downtown into Lady Bird Lake, which is formed by a dam on the Colorado River.

9. Speedway was a city street, now closed through the campus, and a major north-south corridor through the campus. The street presented a major eyesore, a safety concern, and a mobility challenge in the heart of the campus.

10. A good start had already been made on this plan under a grant from the Getty Foundation (UT Austin School of Architecture and Volz & Associates 2011).

11. The need to better understand how space is used on campus persists. In April 2016 the university's president, Greg Fenves, launched such an assessment focused on administrative and library space.

12. Subsequently, Kenney left Sasaki and joined the new San Francisco office of Page (formerly Page Southerland Page). He received master's degrees in both planning and architecture from the University of Pennsylvania and a bachelor's degree in architecture from the University of Colorado. Parsons founded Sasaki Strategies, strategic planning offshoot of Sasaki Associates. He had a lengthy tenure as dean for planning at Harvard's Faculty of Arts and Sciences. He was educated at Cambridge and Harvard Universities. Parsons and Sasaki Strategies pioneered the space management assessment and planning tool at Ohio State University.

13. The dean of engineering, Greg Fenves, later became provost and subsequently university president.

14. Dan Kenney is the coauthor of a book on campus planning, *Mission and Place* (2005).

### CHAPTER 2 — READING LANDSCAPES

1. Officially, the law was titled the Federal Water Pollution Control Act Amendments of 1972. The "amendments" were a complete rewrite of an original 1948 law. The 1972 act significantly expanded water quality authorities.

2. Austin Tomorrow had over 160 pages of laudable goals, objectives, and policies. City planner Garner Stoll argues that these were largely ignored throughout its over thirty-year existence. He notes one exception is its environmental policies, which were implemented through differential parcel-by-parcel impervious surfacing requirements and large-scale open space acquisitions. Stoll's view is that Austin Tomorrow's major

shortcoming was that it was implemented in a fragmented, noncomprehensive manner. Andrew Busch offers another criticism of Austin Tomorrow: that "while well intentioned and more democratic than previous models, it suffered from an inability to address the particular features inherent in Austin's spatial organization and historical patterns of segregation" (Busch 2016, 88).

3. ETJs are a unique Texas authority given to cities to regulate land use outside their city limits. This facilitates annexation, which is one reason Texas cities have grown to be so large.

4. Austin's green building program influenced the design of the US Green Building Council's Leadership in Energy and Environmental Design standards, commonly known by its abbreviation as LEED.

5. According to a 2016 US Forest Service report, Austin's trees provide almost $34 million annually in ecosystem services and benefits to the community in air pollution removal, carbon sequestration, and energy savings and have a value of $16 billion (Nowak et al. 2016).

6. Actually, Robinson presented several versions of his "top ten" lists. He originally wrote the list in 2007, updated it after the 2010 census, and has subsequently revised it. The list cited here is an adaptation of the one he presented to the task force. One of my changes is to use "white," as the census does, instead of Anglo, which is part of the Texas vernacular, but which I find offensive and inaccurate. (See www.city-data.com/forum/austin/1184044-top-ten-demographic-trends-austin.html).

7. https://www.utsystem.edu/chancellor/history-of-the-office.

8. For the record, I do not use the terms "landscaped" or "landscaping." They reduce the good word "landscape" to decoration. For more about the word, see Doherty and Waldheim 2016.

9. The total square feet or meters of a building divided by the total square feet or meters of the site where the building is located.

10. The Main Mall and the South Mall/Lawn are adjacent and sometimes lumped together and called the Main Mall.

11. Littlefield's home is now on the university campus. Apparently, Paul Cret did not think much of the eclectic Victorian house, as he erased it in his 1933 plan.

12. Littlefield's efforts were part of his ongoing strategy to secure the university on its hilltop site. His plans were in conflict with the plans of his rival (who shared his first two names) George Washington Brackenridge, who campaigned for a Colorado River location (called the Brackenridge Tract). Brackenridge was a Union sympathizer and an advocate for women's suffrage who supported education for women and minorities.

## CHAPTER 3 — DETERMINING SUITABILITIES

1. In this context, "we" is not authorial. I was directly involved as the chair of ECT and dean of the UT Austin School of Architecture.

2. I was a member of Senator Watson's working group.

3. However, these centers cannot be built without receiving approval through the cumbersome and time-consuming planned unit development approval process. This might involve any of Austin's sixty-four boards and commissions.

### CHAPTER 4 — DESIGNING OPTIONS

1. Actually, two votes were taken. In the first, the weaker motion was to "pass" the amended draft plan on to the planning commission. It failed 3 for, 21 against, and one abstention. The next motion to "endorse" the plan passed: 21 for, 3 against, and one abstention. As a result, every member voted to approve the plan in one way or the other, except for the individual who abstained. When the 21 to 3 vote was reported at a city council briefing, councilperson Bill Spelman commented that in Austin, "that's unanimous."

2. Two planners responsible for the Healthy Austin element were funded by the US Centers for Disease Control and Prevention.

3. This was opposed by Rick Perry, who was again running for governor. The board of regents' discussion, which was certainly a "fiscally conservative" consideration, was one of the factors that prompted the governor to appoint regents even more supportive of his ideas.

4. Not to be confused with UT's Brackenridge Tract along Lady Bird Lake.

5. See www.wallercreek.org.

6. The actual design of the buildings in the resulting medical district, however, would require a more detailed understanding of site constraints, including the floodplain, existing vegetation, State Capitol viewing corridors, and traffic patterns.

### CHAPTER 5 — SELECTING A COURSE

1. I voted for the map.

### CHAPTER 6 — TAKING ACTIONS

1. Larry Speck was the lead architectural designer for the first medical school building. He and his firm Page (formerly Page Southerland Page) contributed to the design on the research and office buildings as well as the parking garage. Because of the very tight time frame, his experience with campus planning proved invaluable. Speck carried on a tradition of earlier architect-planners who had made campus plans and then designed buildings that helped realize that plan, including Cass Gilbert, Paul Cret, and Pelli Clarke Pelli.

2. SITES resulted from the Sustainable Sites Initiative developed by the Lady Bird Johnson Wildflower Center, the US Botanic Garden, the American Society of Landscape Architects, and others. In June 2015, Green Business Certification Inc. (GBCI) assumed responsibility for SITES. GBCI, formerly the Green Building Certification Institute, is an offshoot of the US Green Building Council.

3. However, given the city's tendencies toward "terminal democracy" and inaction regarding implementation, the code rewrite process dragged on and became costlier. Entering the summer of 2016, the process had been delayed by a year and a half with city council adoption targeted for 2018. Meanwhile, the budget for the rewrite project had grown from $2 million to $2.6 million, heading toward $3.2 million.

4. Subsequent planning and design reduced the number of units in the first phase to

around 575 units but set up the possibility for more housing in the future.

5. In my view, UT Austin functions more like a hybrid Camry—with good gas mileage, relatively low maintenance costs, and great resale value.

6. I believe that enemies of the university underestimated President Powers's resolve. A Vietnam-era veteran, he had served as a US Navy lieutenant junior grade in the Persian Gulf and had the strong support of alumni, faculty, and students.

7. The new medical school received 4,528 applications for the fifty spots in the inaugural class.

8. Sadly, Simmons died on August 31, 2015, before the work was complete, but Bright and Sasaki followed through.

9. I am a former president and board member of the Hill Country Conservancy.

10. Unfortunately, the Lone Star Rail concept was abandoned by local officials in 2016.

## CHAPTER 7 — ADJUSTING TO CHANGE

1. Department of Defense news transcript, February 12, 2002, http://archive.defense.gov/Transcripts/Transcript.aspx?TranscriptID=2636.

2. In February 2016, several citizen and conservation groups, including Save Our Springs Alliance and Friends of the Wildflower Center, filed a lawsuit to prevent the SH 45 and MoPac South projects. The lawsuit claimed that the Texas Department of Transportation and the Central Texas Mobility Authority violated the National Environmental Policy Act by dividing the overall project into three segments to avoid a comprehensive environmental impact statement. The lawsuit noted that the Edwards Aquifer and significant wildlife habitat, including that for the endangered golden-cheeked warbler, would be impacted by the project.

3. In both cases, Todd Schliemann and his Ennead colleagues from New York City.

4. However, parking garages do present a suicide risk on campus, an issue that is being addressed in the design of new garages. Grass and trees adjacent to garages help reduce the risk of suicide.

5. The planner for the Student Life master plan was the Austin firm Barnes Gromatzky Kosarek. The College of Liberal Arts plan was undertaken by PAYETTE and Sasaki.

6. The tunnel design included a major flaw. The intake facility's height violated city and state laws protecting views of the State Capitol. The redesign resulted in increased costs and project delays.

## CHAPTER 8 — REFLECTIONS

1. Martin Luther King Jr., "Beyond Vietnam," speech given April 4, 1967, in New York City, http://kingencyclopedia.stanford.edu/encyclopedia/documentsentry/doc_beyond_vietnam/.

2. Speech at Yale University, recorded in White House Diary, October 9, 1967.

3. The Sasaki team was not involved in the site location of the chilling station.

4. On late Thursday afternoon, August 27, Judge Karin Crump ruled in favor of the university, and the next day the Third Court of Appeals denied the Sons of Confederate Veterans' request for an emergency injunction.

5. The campus planning committee with the help of McKinney/York Architects explored four possible locations and recommended a suitable site near the LBJ Presidential Library and the LBJ School of Public Affairs. President Fenves noted that, as events at Princeton University illustrated, Wilson's racism is a source of controversy as well. As a result, and because Wilson had no direct tie to UT Austin, Fenves decided not to relocate Wilson anywhere.

6. Imagine Austin was awarded the Sustainable Plan Award from the American Planning Association, Sustainable Communities Division.

7. The campus master plan received an Honor Award for Excellence from the Society for College and University Planning.

# REFERENCES

Balcones Canyonlands Conservation Plan Coordinating Committee. 2013. "Balcones Canyonlands Conservation Plan 2012 Annual Report" (January). Austin, TX: Travis County, City of Austin.

Beatley, Timothy. 1994. *Habitat Conservation Planning: Endangered Species and Urban Growth*. Austin: University of Texas Press.

———. 2010. *Biophilic Cities: Integrating Nature into Urban Design and Planning*. Washington, DC: Island Press.

———. 2016. "New Directions in Urban Nature: The Power and Promise of Biophilic Cities and Blue Urbanism." In *Nature and Cities: The Ecological Imperative in Urban Design and Planning*, edited by Frederick Steiner, George F. Thompson, and Armando Carbonell, 264–285. Cambridge, MA: Lincoln Institute of Land Policy.

Berry, Wendell. 2012. "It All Turns on Affection." Jefferson Lecture, Washington, DC. http://www.neh.gov/about/awards/jefferson-lecture/wendell-e-berry-lecture.

Brann, William Cowper. 1898. "The Garden of the Gods." In *Brann the Iconoclast*, vol. 1: 184–187. Waco, TX: Press of Knight Printing.

Briscoe, Danelle. 2014. "Parametric Planting: Green Wall System Research + Design Using BIM." In *ACADIA 2014 Design Agency: Proceedings of the Thirty-Fourth Annual Conference of the Association for Computer Aided Design in Architecture*, edited by David Gerber, Alvin Huang, and Jose Sanchez, 333–338. Cambridge, ON: Riverside Architectural Press.

———. 2015. *Beyond BIM: Architecture Information Modeling*. New York: Taylor and Francis.

Busch, Andrew M. 2016. "The Perils of Participatory Planning: Space, Race, Environmentalism, and History in 'Austin Tomorrow.'" *Journal of Planning History* 15, no. 2: 87–107.

Butler, Kent, and Dowell Myers. 1984. "Boomtime in Austin, Texas: Negotiated Growth Management." *Journal of the American Planning Association* 50, no. 4 (Autumn): 447–458.

Calkins, Meg, ed. 2012. *The Sustainable Sites Handbook: A Complete Guide to the Principles, Strategies, and Practices for Sustainable Landscapes*. Hoboken, NJ: Wiley.

Calthorpe, Peter. 1993. *The Next American Metropolis: Ecology, Community, and the American Dream*. New York: Princeton Architectural Press.

Caro, Robert A. 1974. *The Power Broker: Robert Moses and the Fall of New York*. New York: Knopf.

Cesar Pelli & Associates and Balmori Associates. 1999. *Campus Master Plan: The University of Texas at Austin*. Austin: University of Texas at Austin.

City of Austin. 1980. *Austin Tomorrow Comprehensive Plan*. Austin, TX: Department of Planning.

———. 2009a. Community Inventory Report (December 11). Austin, TX: Planning and Review Department.

———. 2009b. Making Austin: Public Participation in the New Comprehensive Plan (September 24). Austin, TX: Planning and Review Department.

———. 2011. Imagine Austin Comprehensive Plan (Draft, September 26). Austin, TX: Planning and Review Department.

———. 2012. *Imagine Austin Comprehensive Plan*. Austin, TX: Planning and Development Department.

———. 2013. *Imagine Austin 2013 Annual Report: A Way Forward*. Austin, TX: Planning and Development Department.

Commission of 125. 2004. *Report of the Commission of 125*. Austin: University of Texas at Austin.

Corneil, Janne, and David Gamble. 2013. "Ideas per Square Foot." *Planning* 79, no. 2 (February): 22–28.

Cret, Paul P. 1933. *Report Accompanying the General Plan of Development* (January). Austin: University of Texas.

Doherty, Gareth, and Charles Waldheim, eds. 2016. *Is Landscape . . . ? Essays on the Identity of Landscape*. New York: Routledge.

Faga, Barbara. 2006. *Designing Public Consensus: The Civic Theater of Community Participation for Architects, Landscape Architects, Planners, and Urban Designers*. Hoboken, NJ: Wiley.

———. 2014. "Formers versus Zoners: How and Why Communities Shift to Form-Based Zoning." PhD diss., Georgia Institute of Technology, Atlanta.

Federal Geographic Data Committee. 2012. *Coastal and Marine Ecological Classification Standard*. Washington, DC: Marine and Coastal Spatial Data Subcommittee.

Frank, Lawrence, Mark Bradley, Sarah Kavage, James Chapman, and T. Keith Lawton. 2007. "Urban Form, Travel Time, and Cost Relationships with Tour Complexity and Mode Choice." *Transportation* 35, no. 1: 37–54.

Friedmann, John. 1987. *Planning in the Public Domain: From Knowledge to Action*. Princeton, NJ: Princeton University Press.

Geddes, Patrick. 1915. *Cities in Evolution: An Introduction to the Town Planning Movement and to the Study of Civics*. London: Williams and Norgate.

Geddes, Robert. 2013. *Fit: An Architect's Manifesto*. Princeton, NJ: Princeton University Press.

Grossman, Elizabeth Greenwell. 1996. *The Civic Architecture of Paul Cret*. New York: Cambridge University Press.

Grove, J. Morgan, Mary L. Cadenasso, Steward T. A. Pickett, Gary E. Machlis, and William R. Burch Jr. 2015. *The Baltimore School of Urban Ecology: Space, Scale, and Time for the Study of Cities.* New Haven, CT: Yale University Press.

Hack, Gary. 2015. "Designing Cities and the Academy." *Journal of the American Planning Association* 81, no. 3 (Summer): 221–229.

Hegemann, Werner, and Elbert Peets. 1922. *The American Vitruvius: An Architect's Handbook of Civic Art.* New York: Architectural Book Publishing.

Hill Country Studio. 2015. *Toward a Regional Plan for the Texas Hill Country.* Austin: Community and Regional Planning Program, School of Architecture, University of Texas at Austin.

Hough, Michael. 1984. *City Form and Natural Process: Towards a New Urban Vernacular.* New York: Van Nostrand Reinhold.

Jacobs, Jane. 1961. *The Death and Life of Great American Cities.* New York: Random House.

Karvonen, Andrew Paul. 2008. "Botanizing the Asphalt: Politics of Urban Drainage." PhD diss., University of Texas at Austin.

———. 2011. *Politics of Urban Runoff: Nature, Technology, and the Sustainable City.* Cambridge, MA: MIT Press.

Kenney, Daniel R., Richard Dumont, and Ginger Kenney. 2005. *Mission and Place: Strengthening Learning and Community through Campus Design.* Westport, CT: Praeger.

Koch & Fowler. 1928. *A City Plan for Austin, Texas.* Dallas: Koch & Fowler.

Laird, Warren P. 1990. "Paul Philippe Cret." In *The Book of the School: 100 Years, The Graduate School of Fine Arts of the University of Pennsylvania,* edited by Ann L. Strong and George E. Thomas, 72. Philadelphia: Graduate School of Fine Arts, University of Pennsylvania.

Lands, LeeAnn. 2009. *The Culture of Property: Race, Class, and Housing Landscapes in Atlanta, 1880–1950.* Athens: University of Georgia Press.

Larco, Nico. 2016. "Sustainable Urban Design—A (Draft) Framework." *Journal of Urban Design* 21, no. 1: 1–29.

Layzer, Judith A. 2008. *Natural Experiments: Ecosystem-Based Management and the Environment.* Cambridge, MA: MIT Press.

Levinson, Sanford. 1998. *Written in Stone: Public Monuments in Changing Societies.* Durham, NC: Duke University Press.

Lewis, Michael. 2003. *Moneyball: The Art of Winning an Unfair Game.* New York: Norton.

Lynch, Kevin, and Gary Hack. 1984. *Site Planning.* 3rd ed. Cambridge, MA: MIT Press.

Martinich, Al, and Tom Palaima. 2015. "Why Removing the Jefferson Davis Is a Big Mistake" (September 2). *Chronicle of Higher Education.*

Mattson-Teig, Beth. 2015. "Making the Case for More Innovation Districts" (December 15). *Urban Land.* http://urbanland.uli.org/development-business/making-case-innovation-districts/.

McHarg, Ian L. 1969. *Design with Nature.* Garden City, NY: Natural History Press/Doubleday.

McKibben, Bill. 1989. *The End of Nature.* New York: Random House.

McMichael, Carol. 1983. *Paul Cret at Texas: Architectural Drawing and the Image of the University in the 1930s.* Austin: Archer M. Huntington Art Gallery, College of Fine Arts, University of Texas at Austin.

Muller, Brook. 2014. *Ecology and the Architectural Imagination*. New York: Routledge.

Neuman, Michael. 1998. "Does Planning Need the Plan?" *Journal of the American Planning Association* 64, no. 2 (Summer): 208–220.

Nowak, David J., Allison R. Bodine, Robert E. Hoehn III, Christopher B. Edgar, Dudley R. Hartel, Tonya W. Lister, and Thomas J. Brandeis. 2016. *Austin's Urban Forest, 2014*. Newtown Square, PA: US Forest Service.

Owens, Marcus, and Jennifer Wolch. 2015. "Lively Cities: People, Animals, and Urban Ecosystems." In *Oxford Handbook on Animal Studies*, edited by L. Kalof, 542–570. London: Oxford University Press.

Palazzo, Danilo, and Frederick Steiner. 2011. *Urban Ecological Design: A Process for Regenerative Places*. Washington, DC: Island Press.

Paterson, Robert, and Elizabeth Mueller. 2013. "Developing the Next Generation of Scenario Planning Software." In *2013 Sustainability Symposium*. Austin: President's Sustainability Steering Committee, University of Texas at Austin.

Pickett, S. T. A., M. L. Cadenasso, J. M. Grove, Christopher G. Boone, Peter M. Groffman, Elena Irwin, et al. 2011. "Urban Ecological Systems: Scientific Foundations and a Decade of Progress." *Journal of Environmental Management* 92, no. 3 (March): 331–362.

Pope Francis. 2015. *Encyclical Letter Laudato Si' of the Holy Father Francis on the Care for Our Common Home*. Vatican City: Vatican.

Puckett, John L., and Mark Frazier Lloyd. 2015. *Becoming Penn: The Pragmatic American University, 1950–2000*. Philadelphia: University of Pennsylvania Press.

Rahman, Tamanna, Rachel A. Cushing, and Richard J. Jackson. 2011. "Contributions of Built Environment to Childhood Obesity." *Mount Sinai Journal of Medicine* 78, no. 1 (January–February): 49–57.

Rouse, David C., and Ignacio F. Bunster-Ossa. 2013. *Green Infrastructure: A Landscape Approach*. Chicago: American Planning Association.

Ryan, Brent D. 2011. "Reading Through a Plan: A Visual Interpretation of What Plans Mean and How They Innovate." *Journal of the American Planning Association* 77, no. 4 (Autumn): 309–327.

Rybczynski, Witold. 1999. *A Clearing in the Distance: Frederick Law Olmsted and America in the Nineteenth Century*. New York: Scribner.

Sasaki Associates. 2012. *University of Texas at Austin Campus Master Plan*. Austin: University of Texas at Austin.

Schön, Donald. 1983. *The Reflective Practitioner: How Professionals Think in Action*. New York: Basic Books.

Shapiro, Ari. 2015. "'Map' Is an Exquisite Record of the Miles—and the Millennia." Radio broadcast, National Public Radio (December 14). http://www.npr.org/2015/12/14/457411671/map-is-an-exquisite-record-of-the-miles-and-the-millennia.

Simmons, M. T. 2015. "Climates and Microclimates: Challenges for Extensive Green Roof Design in Hot Climate." In *Green Roof Ecosystems*, edited by R. K. Sutton, 63–80. New York: Springer.

Simon, Herbert. 1969. *The Sciences of the Artificial*. Cambridge, MA: MIT Press.

Speck, Lawrence W., and Richard Louis Cleary. 2011. *The University of Texas at Austin: An Architectural Tour*. New York: Princeton Architectural Press.

Spirn, Anne Whiston. 1984. *The Granite Garden: Urban Nature and Human Design*. New York: Basic Books.

Steiner, Frederick. 2008. *The Living Landscape: An Ecological Approach to Landscape Planning*. 2nd ed. Washington, DC: Island Press.

———. 2011. *Design for a Vulnerable Planet*. Austin: University of Texas Press.

Steiner, Frederick, George F. Thompson, and Armando Carbonell, eds. 2016. *Nature and Cities: The Ecological Imperative in Urban Design and Planning*. Cambridge, MA: Lincoln Institute of Land Policy.

Swearingen, William Scott, Jr. 2010. *Environmental City: People, Place, Politics, and the Meaning of Modern Austin*. Austin: University of Texas Press.

Tretter, Eliot M. 2016. *Shadows of a Sunbelt City: The Environment, Racism, and the Knowledge Economy in Austin*. Athens: University of Georgia Press.

Trust for Public Land. 2005–2006. *The Travis County Greenprint for Growth*. Austin, TX: Trust for Public Land.

———. 2009. *The Central Texas Greenprint for Growth: A Regional Action Plan for Conservation and Economic Opportunity*. Austin, TX: Trust for Public Land.

University of Texas at Austin. 2013. *Medical District Master Plan*. Austin: University of Texas at Austin.

———. 2014. *Landscape Master Plan and Design Guidelines*. Austin: University of Texas at Austin.

———. 2015a. *East Campus Master Plan*. Austin: University of Texas at Austin.

———. 2015b. "Task Force on Historical Representation of Statuary at UT Austin, Report to President Gregory L. Fenves." Austin: University of Texas at Austin.

US Department of Commerce. 1928. *A Standard City Planning Enabling Act*. Washington, DC: Government Printing Office.

UT Austin School of Architecture and Volz & Associates. 2011. Preservation Plan for the University of Texas Forty Acres. Austin: University of Texas at Austin.

Wallace, McHarg, Roberts, and Todd. 1976. *Lake Austin Growth Management Plan*. Austin, TX: City of Austin.

Windhager, Steven, Frederick Steiner, Mark T. Simmons, and David Heymann. 2010. "Emerging Landscapes: Toward Ecosystem Services as a Basis for Design." *Landscape Journal* 29, no. 2: 107–123.

Yaro, Robert D. 2012. "Metropolitanism: How Metropolitan Planning Has Been Shaped by and Reflected in the Plans of the Regional Plan Association." In *Planning Ideas That Matter: Livability, Territoriality, Governance, and Reflective Practice*, edited by Bishwapriya Sanyal, Lawrence J. Vale, and Christina D. Rosan, 153–178. Cambridge, MA: MIT Press.

Yaro, Robert D., and Anthony Hiss. 1996. *A Region at Risk: The Third Regional Plan for the New York–New Jersey–Connecticut Metropolitan Area*. Washington, DC: Island Press.

# INDEX

INDEX